THE PET LOSS JOURNALS

The
PET LOSS JOURNALS

How to Find Validation, Comfort,
and Hope After Pet Loss

Published by:

Louise Griffey

Disclaimer
This book is intended to help readers understand and recover from the impact of pet loss. It is not a substitute for personal therapeutic help from a suitably qualified person. The author is not liable for any damage arising from the information contained in this book.

Dedicated with love to Ozzie and Moose, whose presence in my life and absence from it inspired these pages, may your legacy comfort others as it has comforted me.

TABLE OF CONTENTS

INTRODUCTION

As I welcome you to "The Pet Loss Journals," I am reminded of the profound journey that has led me here. My name is Louise, and I am honoured to be your guide through this deeply personal exploration of pet loss and grief. This book was born from my own heart-wrenching experience, which began on October 22, 2019, when my beloved Springer Spaniel mix, Ozzie, died unexpectedly. The pain of his loss was only compounded by the tragic death of my Staffie mix, Moose, just 24 hours later. The circumstances surrounding their deaths were tragic and accidental, but the specifics are less important than the overwhelming impact their loss had on my life. These tragic events, occurring shortly after the end of a long-term romantic relationship, left me feeling utterly heartbroken and alone.

The loss of Ozzie and Moose was more than just a personal tragedy, it was a catalyst for a journey of healing and self-discovery. In the aftermath, I struggled with anxiety, post-traumatic stress, and a grief so deep it seemed impossible to articulate. My world had been permanently altered, and I struggled to navigate this new, emptier reality. It was during this dark period that I turned to journaling as a lifeline. The act of pouring my raw emotions onto paper became a crucial part of my healing process. These journal entries, filled with unfiltered thoughts and feelings, form the heart of this book. By sharing them, I hope to validate the experiences of others who are grieving the loss of a pet. Your pain is real, your grief is important, and your feelings are entirely valid. This is a truth I've come to understand through my own journey, though it wasn't always easy to accept.

In the initial months following my losses, I fell into unhealthy coping mechanisms, trying to outrun my grief through excessive exercise and constant distraction. However, suppressing these feelings only made them grow stronger. It was only when I sought therapy, educated myself about grief, and committed to my own healing journey that I truly began to recover. Through this process, I not only found ways to navigate my own grief but also discovered a deep calling to support others on their pet loss journey. Today, as a certified Grief Recovery Specialist with a focus on pet loss, I am dedicated to helping others find their path through grief. This book is an extension of that mission, a hand reaching out to those who are suffering, offering understanding, validation, and hope. "The Pet Loss Journals" is more than just my story, it's an invitation to acknowledge your grief, to honour your bond with your pet, and to begin your own journey towards healing. As we explore these journal entries together, my hope is that you'll find comfort in shared experiences and strength in knowing you're not alone.

If you feel utterly alone in your grief, if you know deep down that the emotional pain you are feeling is real but feel that few people will understand, then picking up this book is the first step towards feeling seen and heard, validated, and finding a safe space to explore your grief. Pet loss is a profound and often misunderstood form of grief. It's a subject that's frequently shrouded in silence, judgment, and shame. Through this book, I aim to break that silence and shed light on the intense emotions that accompany the loss of a cherished animal companion. Thank you for joining me on this journey. May these pages offer you solace, understanding, and a path forward through your grief.

Chapter 1 —

THE HOLLOW SILENCE

In the days following the loss of a beloved pet, the world can feel unnaturally still. The absence of paw steps, the missing jingle of collar tags, and the lack of a warm body curled up beside you create a void that seems impossible to fill. It was in this hollow silence that I found myself on October 26, 2019, just days after both of my dogs had died. As I sat down that evening, the weight of loneliness pressing heavily on my shoulders, I reached for my journal. I wrote:

Journal Entry - October 26, 2019

It's been a bit lonely today. I've been on my own all day, but I tried to keep as busy as I could. I cleaned the whole car because all the dog hair was upsetting me. It's so hard getting used to my own company.

These simple words, written across the page, captured the raw essence of my grief. Each sentence spoke volumes about the struggle to navigate a world suddenly bereft of the unconditional love and companionship my dogs had provided.

The loneliness I felt was all-consuming. The house, once filled with the sounds of playful barks and wagging tails, now echoed with an emptiness that seemed to seep into every corner. I found myself desperately seeking ways to fill the void, to distract myself from the pain that threatened to overwhelm me. In my attempt to keep busy, I turned to cleaning, a common response to grief. The act of scrubbing and organising can provide a sense of control when everything else feels chaotic. But as I vacuumed the car, removing every last trace of dog hair, I was struck by a wave of guilt. It felt as though I was erasing their presence, wiping away the physical reminders of their existence. The truth is, everyone's grief journey is different. Some may find comfort in preserving these tangible memories, while others, like myself, might initially seek to remove painful reminders. There's no right or wrong way to grieve, only what feels right for you in the moment.

Perhaps the most profound part of my journal entry was the admission of how hard it was to get used to my own company. Our pets often become our constant companions, always there to offer a comforting presence. Their loss leaves us not only grieving for them but also learning to navigate a new reality where we are suddenly, startlingly alone. In my case, this loneliness was amplified by the fact that I was living alone for the first time in my life. The silence in the house was deafening, a constant reminder of the companionship I had lost. This new solitude was daunting and overwhelming, making the grief feel even more intense. In my desperation to avoid sitting with these uncomfortable emotions, I found myself engaging in excessive exercise. Every evening after work, I would embark on long walks, covering 10-15 kilometres. At the time, I believed I was doing something positive for myself, keeping busy and staying active. In reality, I was using these walks as a form of distraction, a way to exhaust myself physically so I wouldn't have to confront the emotional pain waiting for me at home.

Looking back, I now understand that this relentless activity was a form of avoidance. I was suppressing my feelings, distracting myself from the grief that needed to be processed. While society often encourages us to "keep busy" during times of loss, I've learned that this can actually delay our healing. By constantly being on the go, I wasn't allowing myself the time and space to sit with my emotions, to truly feel and work through the grief. If you're reading this and finding yourself in a similar place of grief, know that you're not alone. Your pain is real, and it matters, and it's okay to take the time you need to process it. Whether you choose to journal, talk to a friend, or seek professional support, remember that healing is not about forgetting or staying busy until the pain goes away. It's about finding a way to carry the love you shared with your pet forward, allowing their memory to comfort and guide you as you navigate this new chapter of your life.

In the days and weeks that followed this journal entry, I would learn many valuable lessons about grief, healing, and the enduring power of the human-animal bond. But for now, in that moment of raw emotion, I allowed myself to simply feel, to acknowledge the pain, the loneliness, and the profound sense of loss that comes with saying goodbye to a beloved pet.

The raw emptiness of loss carved through my life in October 2019, leaving me grappling with a pain so profound it seemed to echo through every corner of my existence. In the span of just a few weeks, I experienced not one, but three devastating losses that would forever change my world.

Journal Entry - October 30, 2019

This day last week I buried my two babies Ozzie and Moose. This last month has been the worst month of my life. I felt I was coping after my six-year relationship came to an end but now to lose both of my dogs I feel I have nothing left. My house feels empty. I feel empty. I walked the fields three days after I buried them sobbing, wishing they were with me running around.

The universe has a cruel way of testing our resilience sometimes. Just as I was attempting to process the end of my six-year romantic relationship, life dealt another crushing blow, the loss of both my beloved dogs, Ozzie and Moose. Their absence created a void that seemed to swallow everything whole, transforming my once-vibrant home into an echo chamber of memories. My sense of navigating life at that time was just complete numbness. I was walking around in a shell of how I used to be. It's hard to describe, but I was disconnected from everything, barely existing in a world that suddenly felt foreign and empty. Those first walks in the fields where we had spent countless joyful hours together became pilgrimages of pain. Each step without their excited paws running alongside me felt like walking through a familiar painting where all the colours had been stripped away. I found myself constantly looking over my shoulder, expecting to see them bounding through the grass, their spirits still so present in these spaces we had shared. What I didn't understand then, but came to realise later, was how these losses had layered upon each other, creating a complex tapestry of grief.

The pain of losing my dogs had overshadowed my earlier heartbreak, pushing it deep below the surface where it would wait to be processed years later. Our hearts, in their wisdom, sometimes shield us from feeling everything at once, allowing us to process our grief in phases when we're ready to face each layer. Through time and dedicated personal grief work, those same fields that once brought me to tears became sacred spaces of connection. Now when I visit, I can see them in my mind's eye, running, playing, living their best lives. The pain has softened, transforming into a gentle reminder of the love we shared rather than the agony of their absence. The journey through pet loss is deeply personal and profoundly real. While life will never return to what it was before, there is hope in knowing that the raw edges of grief can soften, allowing us to carry our beloved companions in our hearts without being crushed by the weight of their absence. Taking time to reflect through journaling can be a powerful tool in processing pet loss grief. Writing allows you to explore your raw emotions in a safe space, helping you understand the complex layers of your experience. By putting your feelings into words, you begin to make sense of your journey and validate your grief. These journal prompts serve as gentle invitations to examine your emotions, honour your memories, and acknowledge the profound impact your pet had on your daily life. Through this process, you can gradually move towards healing while keeping your cherished connections alive in your heart.

Journal Prompts:

1. What does silence feel like to you now?

2. How does the numbness of grief feel in your body today?

3. Write about a special place you shared with your pet, what do you see, hear and feel when you visit it now?

Chapter 2 –

THE ROLLERCOASTER OF GRIEF

If you've made it to this chapter, thank you. It means the world to me that you are here, reading these words, finding something that connects with you. This journey of sharing my journal entries is deeply personal, and knowing that it may resonate with others is incredibly meaningful. This is a journal entry from October 31st, 2019 a day that will always be profoundly special to me. October 31st marks the birthday of my beloved spaniel cross, Ozzie. That year, he would have turned nine. I had so many plans to celebrate with him, bringing him to his favourite places, feeding him his favourite treats, showering him with endless cuddles. Instead, I found myself grieving, struggling to fill the emptiness his absence left behind.

Journal Entry - October 31st, 2019

Happy Birthday, my dear Ozzie. Nine today. I hope you are enjoying it up there with Moose. Today has been very difficult. I bought some plants and bulbs for your grave, trying to make it as lovely as I could. I can manage when I'm going, going, going, doing things. But it's when I stop and sit still, that I cry, I ache, I hurt, I grieve, I feel anger. Sitting in this house without you both here is morbid. There is no joy in this house anymore. It is only filled with my tears and sadness. I don't want to give up on life, but the darkness hanging over me and in my heart is too hard to shake off. I need my dogs to get me through this so badly. I miss you both so much.

Reading this entry takes me back to that day, and yet, I find myself feeling grateful. I know that might sound strange, how can I feel grateful when this journal entry is filled with so much pain? But I am. I am grateful for the healing journey I've been on since then, grateful that I no longer cry every time I sit still, that my heart doesn't ache in the same unbearable way. Healing is possible. At the time, my house felt like a place of sorrow, but that was my reality. I realise that you might be in that place now. You might still be struggling to find joy in your surroundings, or you may be further along in your healing journey. No matter where you are, know that it's okay. This space is for everyone. One of the hardest realisations for me was how much I had depended on my dogs' love to get through difficult times. Their unconditional love was a lifeline I didn't fully appreciate until it was gone. Grief has a way of bringing guilt to the surface, why didn't I cherish every single moment more? But that's the nature of grief, it brings out emotions we don't always expect or understand. It truly is a rollercoaster, one with no clear map or timeline.

A sentence from my journal entry stands out to me: *"I can manage when I'm going, going, going, doing things. But it's when I stop and sit still, that I cry, I ache, I hurt, I grieve, I feel anger."* I spent so much time avoiding stillness, and maybe you have done the same. Staying busy feels safer than facing the depth of our grief. But eventually, we have to sit with it. For me, healing began in those quiet moments when I finally allowed myself to feel, to process, and to start moving forward, however slowly. If there's something I hope you take away from this, it's that healing begins when we allow ourselves to pause. Even if it's just for five minutes a day, taking a breath, acknowledging our grief, and choosing one small thing that helps us feel even a little bit better. That could be walking in nature, talking to someone who understands, picking up a new hobby, or starting a journal of your own. Writing became my lifeline, and maybe it can be yours too. That day, I bought plants and bulbs for Ozzie and Moose's grave, creating a peaceful, beautiful resting place in the countryside where I grew up. I did it alone because I needed to, and I found it deeply healing. I planted daffodils and bluebells, flowers that now bloom at different times of the year, reminding me that life continues. It's not just about death and loss. There is renewal, beauty, and joy to be found again, even after the deepest pain.

One of the most challenging aspects of pet loss is returning to work. The workplace becomes a battlefield of emotions, where we must navigate through meetings, conversations, and daily tasks while carrying the weight of our grief.

Journal Entry - November 3rd, 2019

Today is Sunday, and I go back to work tomorrow. I'm nervous that I will break down in work because the grief comes in waves. My chest tightens, I get a pain near my heart, and I start breathing fast and just cry uncontrollably. It's difficult to try and get used to my own company, it's quiet and lonely, and I feel like there is a dark cloud above my head. I've tried to keep as busy as I could today, but there is still an emptiness. The dogs are in my head a lot of the day. I am missing the unconditional love from my dogs today.

The physical manifestations of grief are profound. The tightness in my chest, the pain near my heart, these weren't just emotional symptoms but real, physical manifestations of the deep loss I was experiencing. Like waves crashing on a shore, grief would overwhelm me at unpredictable moments. There's an unspoken expectation in professional settings to maintain composure, to somehow place a band-aid over our grief for those eight hours at work. It feels like climbing a mountain, an overwhelming task when your heart is so heavy. The dark cloud of grief follows you everywhere. It's not just sadness, it's an emptiness that fills every moment. Our beloved pets occupy our thoughts constantly, and this is entirely natural. Sometimes we might feel guilty for wanting even a brief respite from these thoughts, but this too is a normal part of the grieving process.

Society often fails to recognise the depth of pet loss grief. While bereavement leave is common for human loss, the death of a companion animal rarely receives the same consideration. This lack of acknowledgment adds another layer of pain to an already overwhelming experience. If you are experiencing this journey, consider taking time off if possible, whether through vacation days or unpaid leave. This isn't just a suggestion, it's a vital step in the healing process. Processing grief requires space and time to feel our emotions fully, something nearly impossible to do while maintaining professional composure. Remember that your feelings are completely understandable, your pain is real, and taking time to heal isn't a luxury - it's a necessity. The journey through pet loss is deeply personal, and there's no shame in needing time to navigate this profound change in your life.

As I delved into my journal from those early days of grief, I came across an entry that transported me back to the raw emotions of that time.

Journal Entry - November 10th, 2019

I had a dream about Ozzie and Moose last night. I was walking them in the fields near my house. It felt so real. I could feel their fur and see their happy faces. I woke up crying. I miss them so much. I feel so alone without them. They were my constant companions and now they're gone. The house feels so empty without them. I keep expecting to hear the sound of their paws on the floor or their barks when someone comes to the door. But there's just silence. I don't know how to move forward without them. They were such a big part of my life for so long. I feel lost without them.

Reading this entry now, years later, brings a flood of memories and emotions. Dreams about our departed pets are a common experience for many grieving pet parents. They can be both a blessing and a heartache, offering a brief, beautiful moment of reunion, only to leave us bereft all over again when we wake. The feeling of profound loneliness after losing a pet is something many of us experience. Our furry best friends are often our most loyal companions, there for us through thick and thin. When they're gone, it leaves a void that seems impossible to fill. The silence in the house can be overwhelming. We're so used to the little sounds that make up the soundtrack of life with our pets, the click of their nails on the floor, the jingle of their collar, their contented sighs as they sleep. When those sounds disappear, it can feel like the house itself is grieving with us.

I remember feeling so lost without Ozzie and Moose, as if I'd lost my anchor in the world. It's such a common feeling after losing a pet. They give our lives structure and purpose, our days revolve around their needs and routines. When they're no longer there, it can feel like we've lost our sense of direction. Moving forward after such a loss can seem impossible at times. Our pets become such an integral part of our lives that imagining a future without them can be heartbreaking. But it's important to remember that moving forward doesn't mean forgetting. We carry the love and memories of our pets with us always, even as we learn to navigate life without their physical presence. Looking back at this journal entry now, I'm struck by how raw and honest it is. When we're in the depths of grief, it can be hard to see any light at the end of the tunnel. But I want to assure you, if you're in that dark place now, that it does get better. The pain doesn't disappear entirely, but it does become more manageable, and our grief grows with us.

If you're experiencing similar feelings to what I've described here, please know that you're not alone. You have the right to feel the way you do. Show yourself understanding and patience as you navigate this difficult path. Remember, the love you shared with your pet was real, and so too is your grief. Allow yourself to feel, to remember, to cry, and yes, even to smile at the joy your animal best friend brought into your life. In time, I found that my dreams of Ozzie and Moose became less painful and more comforting. They served as reminders of the beautiful bond we shared, a love that transcends the boundaries between life and death. Though they are no longer physically by my side, their spirits and energy live on in my heart, guiding me forward with the same unconditional love they always showed. This is the legacy of our beloved pets, the love they leave behind, forever changing us, forever a part of who we are. And in that love, we find the strength to carry on, to honour their memory, and to open our hearts once again to the joy that comes from sharing our lives with these extraordinary beings.

Journal Prompts:

1. Have you found yourself keeping busy to avoid sitting with your grief? What happens when you allow yourself a moment of stillness?

2. How has your daily routine changed without your pet, and what adjustments can you make to ease the transition back to work?

3. Describe a vivid dream or memory you have of your pet. How did it make you feel, and what emotions did it bring up?

Chapter 3

THE OVERWHELMING GUILT AND TRAUMA

Journal Entry - December 10th, 2019

*I*t's been a month since I wrote and it's been a horrendous month filled with anxiety, pain, hurt, flashbacks, and anger. I have cried every day even though I think there must have been a day that I didn't cry, but there wasn't. I don't miss my ex, it's getting easier to live without him, it's nicer to live without him, but it's a double-edged sword because it's getting harder and harder to live without the dogs. I have no closure from that traumatic day and the intense guilt I feel is only getting worse. Counselling helps but only sometimes, it can't bring them back. When I get the flashbacks my chest gets so tight and I struggle to breathe, that is how Ozzie must have felt. These flashbacks come into my mind at any time of the day and I have to deal with the anxiety attacks. I suppose that's PTSD. I haven't come in contact with a dog in so long it feels morbid to me. A week and a half left of work then a break, a break to get my head together to get some *sort of control of this anxiety. I hope with all of my heart that 2020 won't feel so empty for me.*

The journey through pet loss can be an intensely emotional experience, filled with unexpected challenges and profound grief. In the months following the loss of my dogs, I found myself navigating a complex maze of emotions. The breakup that preceded their death created a confusing contradiction, life was better without my ex, yet unbearably harder without my beloved dogs. The physical manifestations of grief took me by surprise. Panic attacks, anxiety, and flashbacks became unwelcome companions in my daily life. Traditional talk therapy, while helpful for other life challenges, wasn't enough to address the deep trauma of losing my dogs. It wasn't until I discovered cognitive behavioural therapy and specialised pet loss support that I began to understand what was happening in my body and mind.

Shame initially prevented me from speaking openly about my PTSD symptoms and panic attacks. Now I understand these were normal responses to a traumatic loss. The physical symptoms, the tight chest, the difficulty breathing, the sudden flashbacks, were all part of my body trying to process these profound losses. I found myself avoiding dogs entirely, a protective mechanism to shield myself from further pain. Taking time off work became necessary, a vital step in my healing journey. The feeling of losing control over my emotions and reactions was overwhelming, leading to self-imposed isolation.

Through professional help and dedicated grief work, I gradually learned to process these intense emotions. The combination of therapy, grief recovery work, and education about trauma responses became my pathway to healing. While the journey was challenging, it taught me that there's no single "right" way to heal from pet loss. Each person's path is unique, and all feelings, from anxiety to trauma to profound sadness, are important parts of the grieving process. My experience has shown me that while the pain of pet loss can be overwhelming, healing is possible. It requires patience, professional support, and most importantly, self-compassion. Remember, you're not alone in this journey, and seeking help in whatever format feels right for you is not just okay, it's an essential step towards healing.

Journal Entry - February 19th, 2020.

My life so far has been a complete and utter emotional roller coaster. I am aware that I have not been coping well with life in general. There is a massive void in my life and no matter how many kilometres I walk or how many hours I work, nothing changes this void. I am empty without my dogs. I am trying to look after my health as much as possible as my body is all I have left and I love this body. It has endured such pain and such loss and it still gets me up in the morning.

This entry captures the raw reality of my grief journey after losing my gorgeous dogs. The void I describe was all-consuming, an emptiness that seemed impossible to fill. I found myself walking excessively and working long hours, anything to keep my mind and body occupied. It was an unhealthy attempt to distract myself from the overwhelming emotional pain. Looking back, I realise now that I was unable to spend time alone with my thoughts and emotions. The constant movement and busyness were my ways of trying to fill that void, but as I noted in my journal, nothing could change it. This is a common experience for many who are grieving the loss of a pet. We try to return to our normal routines, our normal way of living, but it's simply not possible. The pain is too fresh, too raw.

However, even in the depths of my grief, there was a glimmer of self-compassion. I recognised that I was trying to look after my health, acknowledging that my body was carrying me through this difficult time. I loved my body for its resilience, for getting me up each morning despite the immense emotional burden it was bearing. It's important to note that when I wrote "my body is all I have left," it wasn't entirely factual. I did have friends, family, and other positive aspects in my life. But grief has a way of clouding our perception, making it difficult to recognise or focus on the good things that remain. There were mornings when I didn't want to get out of bed, and some days I didn't and that's okay. It's a normal part of the grieving process. What matters is that I was trying. I remember making an effort to eat nutritious food, making green juices, and fuelling my body with healthy, plant-based options. I didn't want my physical health to suffer while I was struggling emotionally.

Looking back, I can see how far I've come. I now have a greater awareness of how I wasn't dealing with my grief in a healthy or effective way. I was burying and suppressing my feelings, which manifested in my inability to cope with life in general. This is a common experience for many who are grieving a pet. Life becomes difficult to navigate, and tasks that were once manageable suddenly feel overwhelming. If you're feeling this way, please show yourself kindness. You've been through a major loss, and acknowledging that is the first step. I encourage you to start journaling. It doesn't matter what format you use or what kind of paper or pen, just start writing. Express your feelings, the emotions you're experiencing today or this week. Getting those thoughts out of your brain and onto paper can help interrupt the negative narrative in your mind.

When I wrote that I wasn't coping well with life in general, I should have followed up with why. It was because I had gone through the worst, most painful experience of my entire life. More painful than any breakup or family issue I had ever faced. I didn't know how to deal with it, cope with it, or process it. But I did know how to suppress it, push it down, and just get on with things. That's what many of us have learned to do since childhood. If you're trying to prioritise your health during this difficult time, I want to acknowledge how challenging that can be. Trying to take care of yourself while grieving is a monumental task. If there's something you can do to thank your body for getting you up each morning, do it. Whether it's drinking a green juice, going for a walk in nature, taking a long bath, or giving yourself a social media detox, anything to be kind to your body and rest your nervous system, which is likely hypersensitive right now. Remember, you are allowed to feel and be exactly as you are. Be kind to yourself. Your body has endured such pain and loss, yet it still gets you up every morning. Show yourself and your body some compassion, kindness, and self-love. That's what you deserve.

Journal Entry - February 20th, 2020

I am struggling to see my worth in this world, what my purpose is supposed to be because it can't be working in this company. I am depressed. I have been depressed since they died, which is nearly 4 months now. I'm not sure crying is releasing much, but I still do it every single day. I am feeling crippling guilt for putting Moose to sleep. I chose to end her life. My life was centred around giving Moose choice in all she did, and she didn't have that the day she died.

This journal entry highlights a feeling that is incredibly common among those who have lost a pet: guilt. It's probably the most frequently discussed emotion in my pet loss support groups and in my client sessions. The guilt associated with euthanising a companion animal is particularly intense and confusing. When we think about it logically, putting a beloved pet to sleep is an unnatural and deeply challenging act. I've spent countless hours ruminating on this concept, tormenting myself with conflicting feelings of hurt and self-blame. I felt as though I had taken away Moose's choice, her chance to live, even though circumstances left no other option.

You have likely been in a similar position, whether your pet was diagnosed with terminal illnesses, reached the end of their natural life, or suffered accidents leaving them in unbearable pain. Regardless of the reason, the guilt we feel is a testament to our humanity and the depth of our love for these beings who were so much more than just animals, they were our best friends, our children, our whole world. The pain of this guilt can be crippling and difficult to navigate. But as I embarked on my grief recovery journey, I found a simple yet powerful reframe that helped me process these emotions. At its core, guilt implies an intent to harm. When I asked myself, "Did I intend to harm my gorgeous Moose that day?" the answer was a resounding no. I invite you to ask yourself the same question about your own pet. I'm certain you will also answer with a firm "No, of course not."

Instead of guilt, I've learned to say, "I regret the circumstances that led to this outcome." I've found compassion and kindness for myself, trusting that the choice I made was the best one for my girl. Our companions can't verbalise these decisions, but as their guardians, we're responsible for ensuring their quality of life. I encourage you to challenge the narrative you may be telling yourself about guilt. Society has skewed our understanding of this word, often tying it to childhood experiences of wrongdoing. But in the context of pet euthanasia, it doesn't quite fit. What feels more aligned for me is acknowledging the regret around the situation while recognising that I would have done anything humanly possible to keep Moose here on earth if I could have. Take a moment after reading this chapter to close your eyes and reflect. If there was another emotion or word to describe your feelings about your pet's death, would it still be guilt? Or could it be something that better honours the love and care you had for your companion? Here are some prompts that may be helpful:

Journal Prompts:

1. What physical symptoms of grief have you experienced since losing your pet? How do these sensations affect your daily life, and what helps you cope when they arise?

2. Reflect on one small act of self-care you can commit to this week. How might this act honour your pet's memory and support your healing journey?

3. Reflect on a moment when you felt guilty about a decision you made for your pet. How might you reframe that experience using the concept of "regret" instead of "guilt"?

Chapter 4

EMBRACING THE UPS AND DOWNS

As I sit down to write this chapter, I'm reminded of the ups and downs that come with grieving the loss of a beloved pet. It had been nearly a month since my last journal entry, and I find myself in a different emotional space.

Journal Entry - March 17th, 2020

Ups and downs, but mostly ups, thankfully. Letting go of the guilt and being kinder to myself. I have so many positives in my life: my wonderful friends, my supportive family, my beautiful house, my health, my car, my independence, my job, my freedom from hurt. These are only eight things, and these eight things extinguish guilt and are also extinguishing anxiety. I am changing my thought pattern. I am focusing on now and letting go of the residue of the past. I am letting my true path come true. Missing my angels every day.

This entry marks a significant shift in my grief journey. Unlike previous entries that were raw and intense, filled with sadness and what we might call "negative" emotions, this one highlights the positives in my life. It's important to note that these ups and downs are a common part of the grieving process. We don't always feel the same intensity of emotions day after day. In this entry, I identified eight things that were helping to extinguish my guilt and anxiety. While these feelings may not be gone for good, at that moment, I felt more focused on changing my thought patterns around guilt. I had begun to shift the narrative in my mind, particularly around the difficult decision of euthanasia. Letting go of the residue of my past doesn't mean burying or suppressing my feelings. Instead, it's about releasing what's no longer helpful and recognising the positives in my life. This is a crucial step in the healing process. If you're on your own grief journey, I encourage you to take out your journal and write down eight positive things in your life. These could be things that make you feel good, supported, or that help alleviate your guilt and anxiety.

Remember, what works for one person may be different for another, and that's perfectly okay. Being kinder to myself was a significant part of my healing. I realised that I never intended to harm my dogs or do anything hurtful. By acknowledging this, I was able to let go of some of the guilt I had been carrying. I invite you to consider how you can be kinder to yourself today. Is there a particular narrative in your mind that's causing stress and anxiety? Can you change it, even just for today? Writing in a journal, even if it's just on a sticky note or a blank sheet of paper, can be incredibly healing. It's a way to start processing your emotions and experiences. Not every day in grief is filled with tears and intense pain. There are ups and downs, and it's important to recognise and honour both. When I wrote about letting my true path come true, I had no idea what lay ahead. I didn't know I would train in grief education or facilitate pet loss groups. But looking back, I can see how this moment planted a seed for my future path. If there's something you've always wanted to do or a place you've wanted to visit, listen to your gut. Sometimes, our grief can open doors to new possibilities we never imagined.

Journal Entry - April 12th, 2020

I have been missing the dogs so much during this coronavirus lockdown. They have just said three more weeks of lockdown. The whole country has been shut down since the second week of March. It's difficult and lonely, but I need to stay strong because it won't be forever. The two Robins were in the garden again, as they always are. Ozzie and Moose, I think. I'm sure of it. They are gone nearly 6 months. It feels like only two. It hurts so much still, but I'm trying my best. Grief is so... it's horrible. It's torture. I miss my friends and family.

This entry captures a moment of intense emotion, written in the midst of the coronavirus lockdowns. I was grappling not only with the loss of my beloved dogs, Ozzie and Moose, but also with the sudden isolation imposed by the pandemic. Living alone, I found myself cut off from the comfort and support of friends and family, intensifying the already overwhelming experience of grief. The appearance of the two robins in my garden became a source of solace during this challenging time. They first showed up the day after my dogs died, and seeing them perched together brought a mix of emotions. I couldn't help but feel a connection, as if Ozzie and Moose were sending me a sign that they were still with me in spirit. This experience of finding meaning in nature's small wonders is common among those grieving. Many people report seeing birds, butterflies, or finding feathers in unexpected places, interpreting them as messages from their departed loved ones, whether pets or people.

Looking back, I realise how much I was struggling with the concept of "staying strong." I wrote those words as if they were a mantra, a shield against the pain. But now, with the benefit of hindsight and my work in grief recovery, I understand that this idea of needing to be strong is a myth that can actually hinder healing. It's okay not to be strong all the time. It's okay to break down, to cry uncontrollably, to wail and scream if that's what you need to do. True strength often comes from allowing ourselves to be vulnerable, to fully experience and express our grief. The isolation of lockdown heightened every emotion, making the grief feel even more intense. It was an unnatural situation, being told to stay home, cut off from our usual support systems. For those who lost a pet during this time, the experience must have been particularly challenging. But it's important to remember that whether a loss occurred during lockdown or more recently, each person's grief is unique and you have the right to feel and process your emotions. We shouldn't compare losses or think that one circumstance is inherently worse than another.

Pet loss grief is a profound and often underestimated form of mourning. It's real, your pain is a reflection to the significance of what you've lost, and it can be utterly heartbreaking. Remember, in the depths of grief, even the smallest signs of comfort, like my two robins, can offer hope and a sense of connection. These moments remind us that while our beloved pets may no longer be physically present, their love and the bond we shared with them lives on in our hearts.

Journal Entry - April 24th, 2020

It's 2 days after the dog's 6-month anniversary. It was a tough day but also a good day. I bought two plants in the garden shop and planted them in the grave and weeded the grave too. It looks very well now. I sat there for a while and cried a little at the fact that I was able to get on with life for half a year without them, especially Ozzie. I felt them near me for a couple of minutes at the grave. I thought I visualised Oz nudging my elbow and Moose rolling in the grass. I can choose to think of the good times I had with my dogs, not just that one bad day. All the amazing days and years I had should outweigh and overtake that one bad day. Maybe in another few months I'll get there. I know I will when that ache and pain in my chest stops happening and my heart feels a little more healed with time.

Their final resting place has become a sanctuary of peace for me. Under a beautiful tree in my family home, I've created a garden that blooms throughout the year with daffodils, snowdrops, and lavender plants. It's become more than just a grave, it's a place of connection and remembrance. Everyone's place of peace looks different. For some, it might be where they scattered their pet's ashes, a special corner in their home, or even a piece of jewellery containing their pets ashes. What matters is finding that sacred space where you feel closest to them. Looking back at my journal entry now, I realise I was putting unnecessary pressure on myself to focus on the good memories while trying to suppress the pain of that final day. The death of our pets can be deeply traumatic, bringing forth a complex mix of emotions, guilt, anger, and so much more. At just six months, I was still in the depths of my grief, and that's perfectly normal. The intensity often increases around anniversaries and milestones.

I used to believe that time alone would heal my heart, but I've learned that healing comes through actively working through our grief. Simply waiting for time to pass wasn't enough, real healing began when I chose to address my unresolved grief and process it properly. This led me to the Grief Recovery Method®, which I now teach to others who are walking this difficult path. The spiritual connection with our pets can continue even after their physical presence is gone. Those moments when I felt Oz nudging my elbow or saw Moose rolling in the grass were real to me. Whether through signs like visiting birds or quiet conversations with them, these connections can provide comfort during our healing journey. Remember, there's no timeline for grief, and it's okay to still feel sadness even years later. What changes is the intensity and how we carry it.

> **Journal Prompts:**
>
> 1. What are eight positive things in your life right now that help balance the weight of your grief?
>
> 2. Describe a small, unexpected moment or sign that brought you comfort during your grieving process. How did it make you feel?
>
> 3. What physical space brings you closest to your pet's memory? Describe how this place makes you feel and any rituals you've created there.

Chapter 5 –

LOCKED DOWN WITH LOSS

Journal Entry - May 10th, 2020

I am really struggling. I am writing because I want to figure out why. I know I am still grieving the dogs but all of these other feelings are taking over a bit now. I find myself looking in my calendar on my phone quite a lot in a day but that's something I always did but my calendar is wiped empty now. No big cycles, no weddings, no trips away with friends, no weekends visiting family. The only one thing I have in my calendar is a week off in October for the dogs' one year anniversaries where I want to go up to the Cuilcagh Boardwalk Trail again and climb The Stairway to Heaven. My coping strategy to the breakup with my ex was planning things and filling my calendar so that I would always have something to look forward to and not be in my house and now all of that has gone the complete opposite. My coping strategy has been taken away from me and I feel low, really low. This lockdown has fucked with everything and I know things could be a lot worse.

Grief during the pandemic brought unique challenges that none of us were prepared for. The emptiness of my calendar mirrored the emptiness in my heart as I navigated the loss of my beloved dogs, Ozzie and Moose, while isolated from the world. The usual comfort of planning adventures and filling my days with distractions was stripped away, leaving me alone with my raw emotions. The tradition of climbing the Cuilcagh boardwalk trail in Northern Ireland became my anchor, a yearly pilgrimage to honour their memory. It started just months after their passing, and continues to this day, a testament to the enduring bond we shared. The timing of their loss, mere weeks after a difficult breakup, created a perfect storm of grief that felt impossible to process in isolation.

Looking back at my anger during those days, I realise now that dismissing our pain with phrases like "things could be worse" only serves to invalidate our genuine feelings. Every tear shed in solitude, every moment spent missing the comfort of my dogs' presence was real and my emotions were genuine and deserving of respect. The pandemic forced me to sit with my grief instead of running from it, and while that was incredibly challenging, it taught me the importance of creating space for these emotions. If you have experienced pet loss during lockdown, know that your struggle was uniquely difficult. The inability to access our usual support systems, the hugs from friends, the comfort of family, the freedom to seek peace in nature, added an extra layer of pain to an already heartbreaking experience. Now I understand that while keeping busy can keep a sense of routine, it's equally important to allow ourselves moments of stillness, to cry in a hot bath, to walk slowly through nature, to simply be present with our grief. Our pets' love deserves to be felt fully, even when that means sitting with the pain of their absence.

Journal Entry - August 3rd, 2020

On Sunday I made a scrapbook of the dogs' lives. I wrote some little notes in there too. I felt at peace doing it and it was an idea that just came to me. I still have bad anxiety and get triggered by certain things but I am getting there slowly, healing and trying every day to focus on the incredible things in my life. I am much more content living on my own now. I enjoy cooking what I want, having my things where I like them in the house and listening to whatever music I like.

This short entry holds so much emotion and reveals the complexities of grief. Creating that scrapbook was a deeply moving experience. In a world where most of our memories are digital, there was something profoundly touching about holding physical photographs of my beloved dogs. The process of printing these images and carefully arranging them in a scrapbook felt almost foreign, yet incredibly special. As I worked on this project, I found myself transported back to the moments captured in each picture. The sights, sounds, and even smells of those times came flooding back. It was an emotional journey, filled with both tears and smiles. I found myself laughing at some photos, while others tugged at my heartstrings. Despite the mix of emotions, there was an overwhelming sense of peace in this creative act of remembrance. For those of you on a similar journey, I encourage you to consider creating a scrapbook for your departed pet. It doesn't matter if you're not typically artistic, this process is about honouring your memories in whatever way feels right to you. You might include little notes, create collages, or even add your own artwork. The act of putting it together can be incredibly therapeutic.

At this point in my grief journey, nearly a year after losing my dogs, I was still grappling with anxiety and triggers. Seeing dogs that resembled mine or witnessing happy families with their pets could provoke intense emotional responses. Sometimes, I'd find myself needing to escape situations that reminded me too painfully of what I'd lost. The sight of a family doting on their dogs would bring a lump to my throat and tears to my eyes as I remembered my own little family unit that had been shattered. One particularly challenging trigger was encountering irresponsible pet owners. Seeing dogs treated unfairly or put in potentially dangerous situations would ignite a mix of anger and sadness within me. I wanted to shake these pet owners and make them understand how precious and fleeting their time with their pets truly is. Another unexpected and difficult trigger was encountering roadkill while driving. These sights would often lead to panic attacks so severe that I'd have to pull my car over to regulate my breathing. It was as if these tragic scenes transported me back to the traumatic moments of losing my own dogs, triggering vivid and distressing flashbacks.

Seeking help through cognitive behavioural therapy was a crucial step in my healing process. Understanding what was happening in my brain during these triggering moments gave me a sense of control. I learned valuable techniques for grounding myself and managing my responses, which made a significant difference in navigating these challenges. While I was making efforts to focus on the positive aspects of my life, I now recognise that this approach wasn't entirely helpful. By trying to concentrate solely on the good things, I was inadvertently suppressing my difficult emotions rather than processing them. However, amidst the grief, I found unexpected joy in my newfound independence. Living alone allowed me to prioritise my own needs and preferences in a way I hadn't been able to for years. This shift towards self-care was an important part of my healing journey, even as I continued to navigate the intense emotions of loss.

Looking back on this entry, I'm struck by the roller coaster of emotions it reveals. Grief is not a linear process, and there's no set timeline, stages or "right way" to grieve. Your feelings, whatever they may be, are full of meaning. It's okay to acknowledge and express your feelings and they are an important part of your healing journey. To you the reader in the depths of pet loss grief, please know that you're not alone. It's okay to feel overwhelmed, to be triggered by unexpected things, or to have days where joy seems impossible. But I want you to know that healing is possible. You will be able to experience joy again, even as you continue to honour the memory of your beloved companion. Your love for your pet is a beautiful thing, and honouring that love, through scrapbooks, through tears, through memories, is an important part of your healing process.

Journal Entry - August 26th, 2020

What a wonderful birthday I had this day last week, spending time with my close friends. It was hard without the dogs, strange. I was upset, but only on and off. It was also 10 months since they died last week, so I felt quite down that day, the 22nd. But I am also completely in love. Never did I think this time last year that a whole year on, I'd be in love with someone. I was really sick three days ago with a bad vertigo attack, bad nausea, and he stayed by my side the whole time. I don't think I've felt that loved in a long, long time.

This entry captures a pivotal moment in my journey. It was my first birthday without my dogs, and the pain of their absence was still fresh. I remember focusing intensely on the passage of time, counting the weeks and months since their death. Looking back, I realise this hyper-focus might have intensified my grief, but it was part of my process. Amidst the sadness, something unexpected had happened, I had fallen in love. This new relationship came as a surprise, a gift I hadn't anticipated. It's a reminder that even in our darkest moments, life can bring us joy and new beginnings. At the time, I was also dealing with debilitating health issues, migraines, vertigo attacks and severe nausea. These physical symptoms seemed to be a manifestation of the emotional pain I was carrying. Yet, in this new relationship, I found a source of comfort and support I desperately needed. I share this personal experience because I want to offer hope.

When we're in the depths of grief, it's easy to feel like the world is against us, to question why such painful things happen. We can fall into negative thought patterns, unable to see beyond our current pain. But I truly believe that even from our deepest pain, something good can emerge. This doesn't mean that the good things erase our grief or replace what we've lost. My new relationship didn't make me miss my dogs any less. But it did bring light into a dark time, showing me that I could still experience love and joy while honouring the memory of my dogs. Everyone's grief journey is unique. Some may experience multiple losses in a short time, the loss of a pet coinciding with the end of a relationship or the death of a human loved one. These compounded grief events can be overwhelming, but they don't define our future.

If you're in a place of grief right now, I want you to know that good things are still possible. New friendships, deeper family connections, or even romantic love may be waiting for you. But it requires us to be open to these possibilities, to allow ourselves to heal and to hope. It's not about forcing positivity or rushing your grief. It's about treating yourself with compassion and kindness, allowing yourself to grieve fully while also remaining open to the good things life may bring. Sometimes, these gifts come in unexpected forms, a new friend, a job opportunity, or a moment of peace in nature. In my darkest moments, I chose to believe that the love I found was a gift from my dogs. Some might find this notion bizarre, but it brought me comfort. It allowed me to see that love and joy could coexist with my grief, that my capacity for love hadn't died with my dogs but had perhaps even grown. As you continue on your own journey with pet loss, I encourage you to be caring and loving with yourself. Allow yourself to grieve, but also allow yourself to heal. Be open to the unexpected gifts that life may bring, even in the midst of your pain. Your grief is real and valid, but it doesn't have to be the end of your story. There can be love, joy, and new beginnings on the other side of loss. Your journey is uniquely yours, but you're not alone on this path.

Journal Prompts:

1. If your calendar feels empty right now, write about one meaningful ritual or memorial activity you could plan, something that honours your pet's memory while giving you a sense of purpose and anticipation.

2. What creative project (like a scrapbook or memorial) could you make to honour your pet's memory? How might this help in your healing process?

3. Imagine your pet could send you a message of comfort. What do you think they would want you to know?

Chapter 6 –

THE WEIGHT OF ONE YEAR

The week leading up to October 31, 2020, was a deeply emotional one for me. It marked the one-year anniversary of losing my beloved dogs, Ozzie and Moose. As the date approached, I found myself reflecting on the bond we shared and the immense void their absence has left in my life. Losing a companion animal is never easy, and anniversaries like this bring a flood of emotions, grief, love, and bittersweet memories.

Journal Entry - October 31st, 2020

Happy birthday Ozzie, 10 today. Last Thursday was the dogs' one year anniversary and I took a few days off work, so did Steve. I didn't want to go through their anniversary on my own and I was just putting my dinner in the microwave when the doorbell rang and there he was I felt my heart explode he surprised me and arrived a day early, he said he didn't want me to be alone. All along I was more focused on just getting through the 22nd and 23rd of October, I wasn't even thinking about doing something nice to remember the dogs but Steve had thought of all that and that completely amazed me. I guess I was so consumed with remembering the events of that traumatic day and days that I couldn't see past it, Steve bought biodegradable lanterns and we decided to drive up to their favourite beach Thursday evening and headed down to the beach for a walk. We sat on a bench and talked for a while until it was starting to get dark, we let off two lanterns and one of them flew high up into the sky, I felt because they were buried together, that the one lantern that flew high was because their two Souls were combined. We sat on the sand dunes and he held me while I cried, we listened to the beautiful sounds of the waves and the in the moonlit sky I felt at peace in this place. He told me he feels like he knew the dogs so well from learning about them through me and me showing him my videos of the dogs which took me a full year to watch but I'm glad I recorded those videos, it's difficult seeing their movements and behaviours, wishing they were alive again.

Some of my family didn't really acknowledge the anniversary which really hurt. My anxiety has been bad the last few days, coming in waves of course, a feeling of panic, sharpness of breath, tight chest. I try to go out for a walk straight away when I feel it coming on, it does help but I still cry and struggle to slow my breathing. I would love to do more meditation but I need more motivation to do it and as my anxiety increases I would love meditation to be a coping strategy. I'll get there, I think Ozzie and Moose would have been proud of me over the last year, I got out and about as much as I could, I fell in love, the love they always gave me is still in my heart, it's still there. I miss them every single day, it still aches but life without them is more manageable now and I'm starting to remember fun times, I do still get vivid flashbacks but that's trauma for you I suppose I have so much love to give in my heart I know that.

Acknowledging being without Ozzie and Moose for one year was very painful and I wasn't sure how to honour their memory in a way that felt meaningful. I took some time off work to be present with my thoughts and feelings which was so helpful. Steve, who had been an incredible source of support throughout this journey, called to visit me to make sure I wouldn't have to face this milestone alone. I was surprised and touched by his thoughtfulness, he knew how much this day meant to me without me even having to say it. He had planned something special to help me celebrate Ozzie and Moose and navigate the day with love rather than sorrow. He told me he didn't want me to be alone because he understood how hard it can be to relive those moments of loss.

As October 2020 came to a close, I realised something profound: grief is not something you "get over." It becomes a part of who you are, a testament to the depth of your love for a living being who changed your life forever. For me, Ozzie and Moose were those living beings. I really feel this journal entry speaks for itself and re visiting a location so special to me helped me to feel connected to my dogs again, I whispered my thoughts to them while watching the sun setting. Steve held space for me that evening and I felt safe in the arms of this caring human being. Not everyone in my life understood why this anniversary was so significant to me. Some family members didn't acknowledge it at all, which hurt more than I expected. But Steve's thoughtfulness reminded me how important it is to have someone by your side who truly understands, or at least tries to.

If you're approaching a similar milestone for your pet's death, I encourage you to find ways to honour their memory that feel right for you. It could be something as simple as lighting a candle or taking a walk in one of their favourite places. You might release lanterns like we did or create a small memorial in your home or garden. The key is not to suppress your feelings but to acknowledge them openly, whether alone or with someone who supports you. Grief is deeply personal and unpredictable, there's no right or wrong way to navigate it. For me, that evening on the beach was both heartbreaking and healing. It reminded me that while Ozzie and Moose are no longer physically here, their presence is still felt in so many ways, in memories, in signs like robins in my garden, and in the love they left behind. As painful as it can be to revisit those moments of loss, it's also an opportunity to celebrate the incredible bond you shared with your pet, a bond that transcends time and space. Ozzie and Moose will always be part of me, just as your beloved companion will always be part of you.

Journal Entry - November 15th, 2020

It's 10:30 p.m. Sunday night and I've realised that when I'm on my own at the weekends, I'm a little bit of a mess. I've had a list of things that I do, like a checklist for that day and when all of that is done then bang, the anxiety comes, the crying, the panic. I've only just realised that I plan my whole day so that I don't have to be alone with myself, my thoughts or my loneliness. Why can't I be okay on my own? I know I haven't been getting that upset about the dogs as much as before. I still

*miss them. I am grateful for 2020 it brought me so much, the dogs sent
me Steve, I know they did. I need to learn again that it's okay to be on
my own. I don't yet feel complete in my life. I know that this is a new
chapter.*

I sat in the quiet of my home, feeling the weight of the
stillness around me. Weekends had become difficult for me.
Without the structure of work or tasks to fill my days, I often
found myself lost in a whirlwind of emotions. I had a checklist
for the day, things to do, but when those tasks were completed,
a familiar wave of anxiety would crash over me. I realised that
I had been planning my entire day around avoiding one thing,
being alone with myself. Why couldn't I be okay on my own?
Why did the silence feel so unbearable? It wasn't as though I
was crying about Ozzie and Moose as much as I used to, that
part of my grief had softened slightly. But their absence still
lingered in the corners of my heart. I reminded myself to be
grateful for 2020, as strange as that might sound. That year had
brought me so much, including Steve, who came into my life
in ways that felt like a gift from my dogs. I knew they had sent
him to me. And yet, even with gratitude in my heart, I felt
incomplete. It was clear to me that this was a new chapter in
my life, one where I needed to learn how to be okay with being
on my own again.

Reflecting on this moment now, I see how common these
feelings are for grieving pet parents. The thought of being
alone, truly alone with our thoughts and emotions, can feel
overwhelming. Whether we live alone or not, grief has a way

of isolating us from ourselves and others. For me, it wasn't just about missing Ozzie and Moose, it was about what their loss represented, an emptiness that seemed impossible to fill. I struggled deeply with this aspect of grief, this inability to sit with myself without distractions or busyness to mask the pain. It's something I've discussed often because it's such an important part of healing. When we avoid our emotions through constant activity or numbing behaviours, we deny ourselves the opportunity to process our grief fully. And yet, it's so easy to fall into this cycle of avoidance. For many of us, this avoidance becomes a pattern, a way of coping with loss after loss until our lives are filled with unresolved grief. When another loss inevitably comes along, a friendship ending, a breakup, losing a job, it adds to the emotional weight we carry like an invisible backpack filled with stones. We keep piling more in until it feels unbearable.

I've learned that recovery from grief doesn't mean forgetting or moving on, it means taking intentional steps toward healing. It means allowing ourselves to feel the pain without judgment and finding ways to honour our pets while also creating space for joy and peace in our lives again. Looking back at that journal entry from November 2020, I see how much I believed that staying busy would somehow make the pain disappear. But time alone doesn't heal wounds, recovery requires action and awareness. It requires us to face our emotions head-on and find healthy ways to process them. If you're reading this and resonating with these feelings, know that you're not alone. Grief is deeply personal yet universally felt by those who have loved and lost pets who were family members in every sense of the word.

Journal Entry - January 21st, 2021

Today was a good day. I have decided to move in with Steve. I have never been more ready for this. I deserve happiness after deep pain. I truly believe that. It's hard to believe it's 2021, another new year without my gorgeous dogs by my side. I see the two Robins in my garden a lot lately, kind of convinced it's them. It's comforting. I'm not sure I will ever stop missing them but one step at a time.

Looking back at this entry, it's clear how much it took for me to get to that moment of deciding to move forward with such a big change in my life. It wasn't easy, and even now, it's hard to believe how much time has passed since then. The decision to move in with Steve was monumental for me, a leap into a new chapter of life while still carrying the weight of grief from losing my beloved dogs. Big changes like this can stir up profound emotions when we are grieving. For me, leaving behind a familiar space where so many memories were made felt like another loss in itself. My house held so much pain, joy, and everything in between. It was where both of my dogs had died, and their presence was deeply embedded in its walls and garden. Thankfully, this wasn't about leaving that house forever. It was still mine, and I could always return to it whenever I needed to feel their energy or be surrounded by those memories. That thought brought me comfort because that house is more than just bricks and mortar, it's a safe haven filled with love and connection to Ozzie and Moose.

Moving forward was daunting. The fear of more loss loomed large, what if things didn't work out? What if I lost someone else important to me? After experiencing significant losses in life, these fears are natural and understandable. They stem from the deep pain of grief and the vulnerability that comes with opening yourself up again to the possibility of joy and risk. But as I wrote in my journal that day, "I deserve happiness after deep pain." And I still believe that wholeheartedly. Grief doesn't mean we stop living or hoping for better days ahead. It means we carry the love and memories forward while allowing ourselves to embrace new opportunities for happiness when they come our way. I also mentioned seeing two robins in my garden often during that time, and I was convinced they were Ozzie and Moose watching over me. That belief gave me comfort then, and it still does now. Even after moving into a new home with Steve, the robins continued to appear as if reminding me that no matter where I go, the love and energy of my dogs are always nearby.

Grief is not linear, there are no set stages or timelines for healing. Each person's journey is unique, and there is no right or wrong way to navigate it. For me, the pain of missing Ozzie and Moose has softened over time, not because I miss them any less but because their memory now brings more warmth than sorrow. If you're grieving a loss while facing big life changes, know that your grief is a personal and meaningful experience that deserves acknowledgment, whether your feelings are fear, confusion, or even hope for what's next. It's okay to take things one step at a time and trust that happiness can follow even the deepest pain. Healing is possible. Recovery is possible. And while it may feel daunting at times, there is hope on the other side of grief, a hope that allows us to carry fond memories of our pets while embracing new chapters in our lives with open hearts.

Journal Prompts:

1. How would you like to honour your pet's memory on their anniversary? What emotions arise as you consider this?

2. Describe a moment when you felt overwhelmed by loneliness after losing your pet. How did you cope with those feelings?

3. How has grief affected a recent big decision in your life?

Chapter 7

LOVE BEYOND DISTANCE

Journal Entry - March 29th, 2021

*O*ne month in my new home. It has been a bit of a roller coaster, mostly emotional, grieving a lot for the dogs, a sense that I was leaving them behind or leaving their energy. I am so happy with my new life down here exploring the area and I know that Ozzie and Moose are giving me the strength to cope.

This entry marks a significant transition in my life, one that brought unexpected waves of grief and emotion. I made the decision to move an hour and a half away from my home to be with my new partner, Steve. It was a risk, filled with excitement and fear, but one that felt right despite the challenges. What I didn't anticipate was how this move would intensify my grief. I hadn't realised that changing locations, leaving the house where my dogs had lived and died, was itself a loss event. This new chapter added another layer to my grief experience, compounding the pain I was already feeling. The emotional roller coaster I experienced was intense. I felt guilty, as if I was leaving Ozzie and Moose behind, abandoning their memory and the energy they left in our old home. I worried that I might start forgetting things about them, that the cherished memories I held so dear might fade. These conflicting feelings are a normal response to grief, especially when combined with a significant life change.

I struggled with the idea of maintaining my spiritual connection with Ozzie and Moose. The physical aspect of my relationships with Ozzie and Moose may have ended, but the spiritual and emotional bond can live on. I was worried the appearance of the little robins would stop and I feared losing this connection would be the result of moving away from the place we shared. It's important to recognise that these feelings are completely normal when facing a move after losing a pet. Whether you're leaving a rental where your pet's ashes were scattered or selling a house filled with memories, the sense of leaving your pet behind can reignite grief in unexpected ways. During this time, I found solace in journaling. I often wrote directly to Ozzie and Moose, asking for their strength, healing, or comfort. This simple act became a powerful tool for processing my grief. I'd frequently end my entries with "Love you, Ozzie and Moose," as if I was writing them a letter. This practice helped me feel connected to them, even as I embarked on a new chapter of my life.

Journaling doesn't have to be complicated or structured. It can be as simple as putting pen to paper and letting your thoughts flow. Through this experience, I learned the importance of leaning into discomfort and fear. Our pets would want us to be happy and to embrace new adventures. They wouldn't want us to remain stagnant in our grief. This realisation helped me move forward while still honouring the love I shared with Ozzie and Moose. Remember, your pet grief is real and it's okay to express your feelings. Treat yourself with kindness as you navigate these complex emotions. Whether you're facing a move, a career change, or any other life transition after losing a pet, know that it's okay to feel conflicted. Your love for your pet doesn't diminish with distance or time. They remain a part of you, supporting you through every new chapter of your life.

Journal Entry - May 24th, 2021

Today is a beautiful day outside. I am trying to focus on everything I am grateful for today. I just try and accept that I may never get over the loss of my dogs and I may often have anxiety around other dogs. So much of people's conversations when I'm in the company of them and their dogs revolves around their dogs and it's really hard to engage with their dogs. Particularly yesterday I didn't look at their dogs that much. It's just so painful. I know if I don't introduce dogs into my life soon, I may not ever want anything to do with them. The more time that goes on the more and more I really don't want to be a dog parent again. I don't ever want to go through the pain of losing a dog again. Maybe owning Ozzie and Moose was just a section of my life that's not meant to be replaced by another pet. Owning them was magic, it was special, nothing could top that. I want to treasure all of the memories from those years and never forget them and the intense love they gave me. I'm okay with not being a dog parent again.

Maybe I might volunteer at a rescue centre in a month or two that might be nice.

Reading this entry now, years later, I'm struck by the sadness that is imbedded in every word. It's a stark reminder of the intense pain and confusion that follows the loss of a beloved pet. I want you to know that these thoughts and emotions are entirely normal and common. If you're experiencing similar feelings, please don't judge yourself harshly. What stands out to me now is how many grief myths I had internalised at that time. The idea that I needed to "get over" the loss of my dogs is a prime example. This notion, so prevalent in our society, is actually harmful and unrealistic. The truth is, you never truly "get over" the loss of a loved one, whether human or animal. Instead, you learn to live with the loss, integrating it into your life story. The anxiety I felt around other people's dogs was overwhelming. Being in situations where I had to interact with pets or listen to others talk about their furry companions was incredibly painful. It felt like a constant reminder of what I had lost, of the joy I feared I'd never experience again. If you're feeling this way, know that it's okay to set boundaries and avoid situations that feel too painful. My reluctance to consider owning another dog was a form of self-protection.

When we experience a profound loss, it's natural for our brains to try to shield us from future pain. The thought that "I don't ever want to go through the pain of losing a dog again" is a common reaction. It doesn't mean you'll feel this way forever, but it's important to honour these feelings when they arise. Looking back, I can see how I struggled with the idea of "replacement." The belief that Ozzie and Moose were irreplaceable led me to think I could never open my heart to another pet. While it's true that no pet can ever replace another, each relationship is unique, this doesn't mean we can't form new, meaningful bonds in the future. The conflicting feelings are evident in my journal entry. On one hand, I was closing myself off from the idea of ever having another pet. On the other, I was considering volunteering at a rescue centre. This internal struggle is a normal part of the grief process. It's okay to have these contradictory thoughts and feelings.

Now, years later, I can say with certainty that I no longer believe in these grief myths. Through education and personal growth, I've learned to understand and process my grief in healthier ways. I'm now comfortable around other dogs, and I don't constantly ruminate about my loss when I'm with animals. I've come to believe that Ozzie and Moose were in my life for exactly the right amount of time, even though their deaths were traumatic and I would have them back in a heartbeat if I could. This shift in perspective has brought me comfort and allowed me to appreciate the time we had together without being consumed by the pain of their loss. The experience of losing Ozzie and Moose has led to what some might call post-traumatic growth. While the term can be controversial, it resonates with me. The personal and professional growth I've experienced as a result of my loss has been profound and unexpected. It's what drives me to share my experiences and help others navigate their own pet loss journeys. If you're in the midst of grief right now, know that there's no timeline for healing. Growth may come, or it may not, and both are okay. What's important is that you allow yourself to feel your emotions fully and seek support when you need it.

Journal Entry - June 5th, 2021

I'm struggling to write because I'm crying. I can't understand how painful this grief is. How can I help myself heal after the death of my dogs? Could I talk more about them? Could I talk about them less? What have I tried? What has worked with my healing? What haven't I tried? Could I try reminders, affirmations when I feel waves of grief? Hiking helps with my grief but my promise to myself of doing one hike every weekend hasn't happened. It's a recurring feeling of doing a tough hike that helps to heal even some of the pain from the grief. I feel that the dogs are with me when I hike. I feel emotional at some stages of it and when I hike alone I feel such a sense of achievement and I feel some of the strength that used to be inside me coming back. This is something that I've sidelined since I've been in a relationship and it's part of my life that I want back and if it means sacrificing some quality time for my mental health then surely it's worth it. It's like I have this built up grief energy that I just need to release. I need to do this. I need to do this one hike every weekend. Just do it for you Louise. My poor babies, I miss you both. It's unbearable. I wish I could see you both again.

Reading this entry now, I'm struck by how accurately it captures the ebb and flow of grief. The waves of sorrow that wash over us, sometimes unexpectedly, are a common experience for those mourning a cherished pet. I want you to know that if you're still feeling intense grief long after your pet's death, it's completely normal. There's no set timeline for healing, and your feelings are valid no matter how much time has passed. In my journal entry, I was desperately searching for ways to process my pain. I was asking myself so many questions, trying to understand why the grief was still so raw nearly two years after losing my dogs. Looking back, I can see the pressure I was putting on myself to "figure it out," as if there was a simple solution to ease the heartache. One thing that clearly helped me was hiking. Being in nature, climbing mountains, and feeling close to my dogs in those moments was incredibly healing. I would often get emotional during these hikes, and now I understand that this was my way of processing some of the grief and trauma associated with their loss. It's interesting to note how entering a new relationship had caused me to sideline this crucial coping mechanism. This is a common occurrence in life, we sometimes neglect the very things that bring us solace and strength when we become engrossed in new experiences or relationships. But recognising this and making a conscious effort to reclaim those healing activities is an important step in the grieving process. Solo hiking, in particular, was a powerful tool for me.

While it's important to be mindful of safety, especially in challenging weather conditions, there's something uniquely therapeutic about being alone in nature. It allowed me to connect with my feelings without distractions, to be present with myself and with the energy of my dogs that I felt around me. I encourage you to reflect on your own life. Is there something you used to do that helped you cope with grief waves? Have you stopped doing it? Or is there a new activity you'd like to try? It doesn't have to be hiking, it could be sea swimming, beach walks, forest bathing, or any form of connecting with nature. The key is to find a way to be still and present, away from the constant distractions of screens, work, and daily responsibilities.

Even if you're struggling to get out of bed due to overwhelming grief, try to take small steps. A short walk outside your house or a brief visit to a nearby park can be a start. It's not about distracting yourself from the grief, but about finding a way to release some of the unresolved sorrow that's trapped inside your body. During my hikes, I would often become emotional at unexpected moments. Instead of questioning these feelings, I learned to accept them as part of the healing process. I allowed the tears to flow freely, recognising that this release was exactly what I needed.

It's important to remember that crying is a natural and healthy response to grief. Never apologise for your tears or feel ashamed of your emotions. They are a testament to the love you shared with your pet and an important part of the healing path. In my efforts to maintain regular hikes, I realised that setting overly ambitious goals wasn't always realistic. Instead, I focused on getting out in nature daily, even if just for a short walk. The benefits of this simple practice have been incredible for my mental and physical health. I've noticed a significant improvement in my overall well-being since making outdoor time a priority. For instance, I used to suffer from debilitating vertigo attacks that would leave me bedridden for days. During these episodes, I deeply missed my daily nature walks, and this absence profoundly affected my mental health. When I finally recovered and could resume my outdoor routine, the positive impact on my mental state was remarkable.

It's worth noting that these vertigo attacks began around the time I experienced multiple losses in my life, including the deaths of my dogs. As I started to process my grief more effectively, the frequency of these attacks decreased. This experience highlighted for me the deep connection between our emotional well-being and physical health. Grief can manifest in our bodies in various ways, through illness, accidents, or other physical symptoms. It's a powerful reminder of how interconnected our minds and bodies truly are. The concept that "the body keeps the score" resonates deeply with many who have experienced loss and subsequent health issues. As you continue on your own journey of pet loss grief, I encourage you to explore ways to connect with nature and with yourself. Find activities that allow you to release emotions and be present in the moment. Whether it's exercise, outdoor adventures, or quiet contemplation, honour what feels right for you. Handle yourself with care as you navigate this challenging path. You're not alone in this journey, and there is hope and healing ahead.

Journal Prompts:

1. If you could write a letter to your pet about the changes in your life since their death, what would you want them to know?

2. How has your perspective on pet ownership changed since your loss? What fears or hopes do you have about potentially welcoming another animal into your life?

3. What is one activity or hobby that has helped you cope with your grief? How has it impacted your healing process? If you haven't found one yet, what would you like to try?

Chapter 8 –

$$\text{---}\,\diamond\!\!\!\!\!\!\diamond\,\text{---}$$

TRIGGERS AND TURMOIL

Journal Entry - June 20th, 2021

I *am struggling a lot. I don't seem to be going forward with my healing. The trauma is more real than ever. I think I need to see someone that can help with this PTSD. I want to work on a solution so that I can get back in control of my life. I don't want to push Steve away. I don't want to lose him either. I'm being triggered so much more lately and it's like I'm hyper sensitive and on high alert. I just want to look at and be around dogs and not see my dead dogs in my head. That's all I want, and I want to stop reliving that awful day.*

Reading this entry now, I can still feel the raw emotion that poured out of me that day. The pain was so vivid, so real. I was experiencing something that I had never heard anyone talk about before - post-traumatic stress disorder (PTSD) from the loss of a beloved pet. It felt isolating, as if I was the only one going through this intense emotional turmoil. The way my dog Ozzie died was traumatic, leaving me with graphic images that haunted me day and night. I found myself trapped in a cycle of flashbacks, both emotional and visual. The area where it happened became a trigger, causing me to freeze in time, feeling numb and disconnected from reality. It was as if my heart, my head, and my soul were transported back to that awful day, reliving the pain over and over again. These episodes often led to panic attacks, leaving me feeling dissociated from my body. I worried constantly that my PTSD would strain my relationship with my partner, Steve. The fear of losing him on top of everything else I was dealing with only added to my stress and anxiety.

My nervous system was in constant overdrive, stuck in a fight-or-flight response that left me exhausted and on edge. The most heartbreaking part was not being able to look at other dogs without seeing the image of my own deceased dogs in my mind. It was a constant, painful reminder of what I had lost. Looking back, I'm grateful that I no longer experience these symptoms with the same intensity. Through a lot of inner work and professional help, I've been able to heal and grow. But I know there are others out there who are still in the midst of this struggle, and my heart goes out to you. If you're experiencing similar symptoms, please know that you're not alone. It's important to understand that PTSD following pet loss is very real and intense. Don't dismiss your feelings or try to minimise them. Seek help from a mental health professional or cognitive behavioural therapist, who can help you understand what's happening in your brain and provide tools to cope.

For me, cognitive behavioural therapy was incredibly helpful in understanding the science behind what I was experiencing. It made me feel less crazy and more in control. Later, completing a pet loss grief recovery program was the final piece of the puzzle, helping me break free from negative thought patterns and reduce my PTSD symptoms. Throughout this process, I encountered well-meaning people who tried to comfort me with phrases like "Don't feel bad, he's in a better place now" or "At least she didn't suffer." While these words were intended to help, they often felt dismissive of the deep bond I shared with my dogs. The suggestion to "just get another pet" was particularly hurtful, as if my beloved companions were easily replaceable. It's important to recognise that everyone's grief journey is unique. While some people may find comfort in welcoming a new pet soon after a loss, others need more time to heal. There's no right or wrong way to grieve, and it's crucial to honour your own feelings and timeline. If you're struggling with PTSD symptoms related to pet loss, please don't suffer in silence. Reach out for help, whether it's to a professional, a support group, or trusted friends and family. Your grief is real, your pain is valid, and you deserve support and understanding as you navigate this difficult journey.

The days leading up to the two-year mark of losing my dogs had been heavy. Looking back at my journal entry from August 2021, I am reminded of just how much grief can linger, even when life continues to move forward.

Journal Entry - August 26th, 2021

Today I am struggling a little. It's always hard being alone in my house. I always seem to think about the dogs. I miss them terribly, especially Ozzie, my boy, my little Heartbreaker. I'm so hard on myself all of the time about the pet loss grief, but I have absolutely no idea when I am going to feel better. The CBT is helping a little. No matter how much love Steve shows me, I still have this emptiness, this immense loss. It hurts. It's draining.

Reading this entry brings up so many emotions. Losing both Ozzie and Moose within 24 hours of each other remains one of the most painful experiences of my life. Each relationship was unique, and each loss hit me differently. Ozzie was with me for nearly nine years and moved through so many life changes with me, moving countries, changing homes, navigating relationships. He was my steadfast companion through it all. Moose was with us for four years and had her own special place in our lives, especially with my partner at the time, who had a particularly close bond with her. It's important for me to acknowledge that it's okay to grieve differently for each pet. My bond with Ozzie was deeply rooted in our shared journey and the challenges we overcame together. Moose, on the other hand, taught me patience and trust as I worked to help her heal from the fear and trauma she carried before joining our family. Both relationships were precious in their own ways.

I've often been hard on myself about this grief, wondering why it still feels so raw after all this time or why I seem to miss one pet more on certain days. But grief isn't linear, and it doesn't follow a set timeline. Cognitive Behavioural Therapy (CBT) has been a lifeline for me during this time, helping me understand the physiological and emotional responses tied to my grief and trauma. It's given me tools to navigate those moments when the pain feels overwhelming. Even with Steve's love and support, there's an emptiness that remains, a void that no relationship can fill because it's not about replacing what was lost, it's about learning to live alongside that loss. For a long time, I tried to suppress my grief, especially when starting a new relationship. Falling in love brought joy into my life again but didn't erase the pain of losing Ozzie and Moose. It took me years to finally sit with that grief and begin processing it fully. I've also struggled with being labelled as "too sensitive" throughout my life, a comment that often felt like criticism rather than understanding. But sensitivity is not a weakness, it's a strength that allows us to connect deeply with others and feel life in all its intensity. Therapy has helped me embrace this part of myself rather than suppress it. Losing Ozzie and Moose changed everything for me. It forced me to confront not only their absence but also how I treat myself during challenging times. If you're reading this and feeling hard on yourself for grieving too much or too long, please know you're not alone. Grief is valid, it's messy, unpredictable, and deeply personal. Take a moment today to be kind to yourself. Wrap your arms around yourself and say: "I'm doing the best I can." Because you are.

Journal Entry - September 18th, 2021

Today, while on my usual walk in the countryside, I encountered something that shook me to my core. I was heading home when I heard the sound of a quad bike approaching from behind. As it passed, I saw a farmer driving with his dog running alongside. The dog looked exactly like my beloved Ozzie. My mind raced, "Will I see this dog every time I walk? It's going to be so painful. It reminds me so much of Ozzie running in the fields." Suddenly, I was back in my garden, vividly recalling Ozzie's lifeless body. Anxiety and fear overwhelmed me. My chest tightened, muscles tensed, and breathing quickened. A panic attack gripped me for 5-10 minutes. I felt short of breath, I was trembling, and crying uncontrollably. I had to stop walking, bent over with my hands on my knees. I wanted to call Steve but couldn't. Eventually, I managed some deep breaths and slowly made my way home.

This entry was part of an exercise my CBT therapist had given me. The goal was to document triggers, my thoughts and beliefs, the consequences (emotions, physical sensations, and behaviours), and then consider alternative thoughts I could have had. Looking back, I wonder if I might have interpreted this differently at a different stage in my grief journey. Could it have been a sign from Ozzie, a little gift to say he's still watching over me?. The alternative thoughts that I could have had around the situation were: "It's natural to notice similarities between dogs. While that particular dog wasn't Ozzie, it's perfectly valid to feel emotional about it. The unexpected appearance of the dog startled you, which is a normal reaction. It's heartwarming to see the farmer enjoying his companion's company as they run together. Memories of

Ozzie's death may surface, and that's okay. Remember, that traumatic event is in the past, not the present. You're safe now, and Oz is no longer suffering, he's at peace." It's strange that I've never seen that dog again, which is unusual for my small, familiar community. This experience taught me the power of journaling through triggers. If you find yourself overwhelmed by similar situations, I highly recommend this exercise. Write down the trigger, your thoughts and beliefs, the consequences (emotional, physical, and behavioural), and then try to formulate alternative, more balanced thoughts.

It's important to remember that not everyone experiences PTSD or panic attacks with pet loss, and that's okay. Whether you do or don't, your grief is unique to you and is experienced in many different ways. There's no set number of symptoms you're "supposed" to experience. Over time, I developed strategies to cope with triggers. For instance, I kept essential oil rollerballs in my bag. During a panic attack, I'd apply these to my wrists, temples, or under my nose. The familiar scents helped ground me in the present moment, reminding me that I was safe and the traumatic event wasn't happening again. Other helpful techniques include naming five things you can see around you, identifying smells in your environment, or keeping a small object to hold, like a stress ball or a crystal. These sensory experiences can help bring you back to the present when memories threaten to overwhelm you. I share these experiences and techniques with you in the hope that they might offer some comfort or practical help. Remember you're not alone, and healing is possible, even if the path isn't always straight or easy.

Journal Prompts:

1. Think about a time when someone's words about your pet loss were unhelpful or hurtful. How did it make you feel, and what would you have preferred they say instead?

2. In what ways have you been hard on yourself about your grief? Write a compassionate letter to yourself, acknowledging these feelings and offering the kindness you'd give to a friend in the same situation.

3. Think about a moment when something reminded you of your beloved pet and brought up strong emotions. What was the trigger, and how did it make you feel physically, emotionally, and mentally? Write about the experience in detail and explore any alternative thoughts or perspectives that might help you reframe it.

Chapter 9 –

THE POWER OF CONNECTION

I'll never forget the moment I stumbled upon this journal entry. It was from September 22, 2021, and it caught me completely off guard. I had no memory of ever writing it, which made reading it all the more emotional. Tears welled up as I realised just how much my life had come full circle since then. Here's what it said:

Journal Entry - September 22nd, 2021

It's difficult to contemplate that the dogs will be dead 2 years next month. The pain is still as raw as it ever was. I wish someday I could set up a group that people can get together to talk openly about their pet grief. To give people a space to cry and to feel their emotions about the trauma and grief would be something so special. Maybe someday. You never know. Love you and miss you, Oz and Moose.

Even now, reading those words feels surreal. At the time, I had no idea what lay ahead or how significant that fleeting thought would become in my life. It wasn't a plan or even an idea yet, just a wish scribbled down on paper in a moment of raw grief. Fast forward to today, and that little spark of hope has grown into something I could never have imagined back then. In early 2023, after months of reflection and healing, I launched an Instagram page for my small business, _lightafterloss. It began as a way to share my own journey through pet loss and to raise awareness about how isolating and unspoken this kind of grief can be. I wanted to create a space where others who felt lost and alone could find support.

Before that Instagram page came to life, though, there was a pivotal moment in the summer of 2022 when I completed my own grief recovery work surrounding the loss of Oz and Moose. That process changed everything for me. Through the Grief Recovery Institute's certification program I learned how to process my pain on a deeper level than I ever thought possible. It went beyond traditional therapy methods like CBT, it brought me peace and acceptance in ways I hadn't dared hope for. That healing inspired me to help others in the same way. By January 2024, Light After Loss had grown into something truly incredible. What started as a deeply personal journey became an opportunity to connect with grieving pet parents across Ireland and beyond. I've worked with clients from all over the world: Germany, France, the U.K., the U.S., and more. Each session has been a reminder of just how universal this pain is and how transformative it can be to share it with someone who understands.

Looking back at that journal entry now feels almost magical because everything I wrote about has come true in ways I couldn't have dreamed of at the time. The group I longed to create? It exists now, not just as an idea but as a real, tangible space where people can cry openly, share their stories, and feel seen without judgment. When Ozzie and Moose died, I searched desperately for something like this, a place where I could talk about my emotions without fear of being dismissed or misunderstood. Instead, what I found was silence, no acknowledgment of how deeply pet loss can affect us physically, mentally, and emotionally. My grief manifested in ways I didn't expect, PTSD symptoms, panic attacks, migraines, and yet there was so little support available for what I was going through. That's why Light After Loss means so much to me. It's not just a business, it's a lifeline for people who feel like they're drowning in their grief. Whether they're dealing with sleepless nights, overwhelming anxiety, or simply struggling to get through each day without their beloved companion by their side, I'm here for them because I've been there myself.

What makes this work even more special is that it's entirely online. Grief can make even simple tasks, like getting dressed or driving somewhere, feel impossible. By offering support virtually, clients can join sessions from the comfort of their own homes, whether they're curled up on the couch in pyjamas or sitting quietly at their kitchen table with a cup of tea. In these sessions, there's no need to apologise for tears or hide emotions behind a brave face. Crying is encouraged, it's part of grieving and healing. For me personally, crying has always been relieving, a way to release pent-up emotions and regulate my nervous system. It's not something to be ashamed of, it's something to embrace. Of course, not everyone grieves through tears, and that's okay too. Grief looks different for everyone, but what matters most is having a safe space where those feelings can be expressed freely. So here we are today, years after I wrote that journal entry and everything has come full circle in ways I never expected but am endlessly grateful for. From the depths of my own heartbreak over losing Oz and Moose came this incredible light, an opportunity to help others find hope and healing after their own losses. If there's one thing I've learned through all of this, it's that our pain doesn't have to define us, it can transform us if we let it. And sometimes, out of the darkest moments in our lives comes something truly beautiful: connection, understanding, and yes, light after loss.

I want to share a personal experience from my journey through pet loss. It's a journal entry from October, 2021, just days after the second anniversary of losing my beloved dogs, Ozzie and Moose. This entry captures the raw emotions and the small acts of kindness that helped me navigate this difficult time.

Journal Entry - October 26th, 2021

It was the dogs' anniversaries last Friday and Saturday and it was very difficult, a roller coaster of emotions. Friday was difficult, it was almost like I was reliving the day again in my head. Driving home for lunch crying but this time Steve saw me driving in and opened the front door so I was met with the love of my life greeting me and that small little gesture made a massive impact on my thoughts. I was upset at lunch but I let it all out on his shoulder while he just held me. There was no judgment or shame, just love. He picked me up from work and we just drove straight up to the beach. When we got there I went to open the boot of the car to put on my boots and there were two white and pink roses lying there. He said 'I thought it would be nice to let them float into the sea in memory of the dogs.' I just couldn't believe he had thought to do such a kind thing for me and for the dogs. We had a lovely stroll together along that beautiful beach and I let the roses float into the water together. Every time I go to that beach I can almost feel the energy of Ozzie and Moose because I truly believe that is where they absolutely loved to go. They were so happy when I brought them there and I like going somewhere remembering their happiness, their excitement and fun. We took some beautiful pictures before the sun went down. The one thing I've learned is that what happened to me was traumatic and real and awful and it's fine not to be healed from it. Just accept that some people don't understand or care very much but that's okay because others, the ones in my life that do care very much, my friends, my partner, I am lucky to have their support. The feelings in the house and back garden will change over time. I just have to be patient and gentle with myself. Loss is incredibly painful but it's only been 2 years. I miss you so much my beautiful dogs.

This entry holds a special place in my heart. It marks a turning point in my grief journey, where I began to celebrate the lives of Ozzie and Moose, rather than solely focusing on the pain of their loss. The simple act of Steve bringing roses to float in the sea touched me deeply. It showed me that even someone who had never met my dogs could understand and honour their memory. Over the years, this beach visit has become a cherished tradition. Each anniversary, we return to this beach, doing something different yet always special to celebrate Ozzie and Moose. These moments allow me to connect with their energy, to cry, to smile, and to feel their presence around me. I've learned that healing isn't linear. Two years after their death, the pain was still raw, the memories still vivid. But I was beginning to understand that it's okay not to be "healed." What happened was traumatic, real, and awful. Accepting this truth was a crucial step in my journey.

I've also come to realise the importance of having supportive people around you during grief. Not everyone will understand the depth of your loss when it comes to a pet, and that's okay. What matters is cherishing those who do offer support and understanding. This experience taught me to be patient and gentle with myself. I had to stop being so hard on myself for not "getting over it" quickly. Grief doesn't have a timeline, especially when it comes to the loss of beloved pets who were such an integral part of daily life. Now, as I reflect on this journey, I see how far I've come. I can celebrate the joy Ozzie and Moose brought into my life, even as I continue to miss them. To you on your own pet loss journey, remember that your grief matters. Find your safe people who truly listen to and support you, and don't be afraid to create your own rituals to honour your pet's memory. Your love for them is eternal, and it's okay to take all the time you need to navigate this loss.

Journal Entry - November 3rd, 2021

I've just noticed that I've been writing in this journal for nearly two years. I'm kind of proud of myself for doing that. Though I definitely feel things are getting better with my PTSD since I've been having CBT sessions, I've been able to understand what happens in my brain when I experience certain things that remind me of the day the dogs died. I now know that my brain is reverting back to that very day, and my body is feeling extreme panic. They are episodes, but now I can come out of them quicker. I do some deep breathing exercises when I can, and if Steve is there, his hugs help too. I know I might never be fully healed from the trauma, but I do think I've accepted that now, and I'm okay with that. I know when I get the anxiety or panic attacks that it's from what happened that day, but I keep telling my brain: "That's not happening right now. You are safe." Every time I look out the window of my home here, I feel so grateful and also in disbelief that I am actually living in this beautiful part of Ireland. My heart just fills up with happiness. I am respected by my partner. I feel safe and secure. I can be myself. Things are great, and they will be better. I am finally adjusting to life without the dogs, and this is a new life now, another chapter of my life. I don't have to let go of the dogs, I just have to remember that their healing energy is around me, and if I need them, I can ask them for their help.

Reading back on those words now fills me with a bittersweet sense of empowerment. It reminds me how important it was to understand what was happening inside me during those moments of panic or anxiety, how my brain was simply reacting to trauma stored deep within me. Learning about PTSD through therapy didn't erase those feelings overnight, but it gave me tools to manage them: breathing exercises, grounding techniques, and leaning on Steve when his presence could calm me. That entry also captured a turning point in my healing journey, the realisation that full recovery from trauma might not be possible and that it was okay to carry some scars forward with me. Accepting this truth didn't mean giving up, it meant finding peace in knowing that healing isn't about erasing pain but learning how to live alongside it. Life at the time felt like a mix of chaos and beauty. There were moments when grief still hit hard, an ache in my chest when memories of Ozzie and Moose surfaced, but there were also moments of joy and gratitude as I adjusted to this new chapter in my new home. Writing down what made me happy became a way to anchor myself amidst the waves of emotion.

I struggled with guilt on days when happiness found its way into my heart. How could I laugh or feel joy when Ozzie and Moose weren't here? But over time, something shifted inside me, a quiet understanding that my dogs would want me to live fully again, to smile, love, and embrace life's beauty without hesitation. Grief has a way of reshaping us, forcing us to reevaluate what matters most in life. For me, it illuminated areas where change was needed, relationships that no longer served me, boundaries that needed strengthening, and self-worth that deserved nurturing. Loss became a teacher in ways I never expected. Even now, as grief occasionally resurfaces or triggers catch me off guard, I remind myself, It's okay to feel everything deeply, to cry when sadness comes but also to laugh when joy returns. Healing isn't linear or perfect, it's messy and unpredictable, but through personal grief work and reflection, I've learned to embrace both the pain and the beauty of this journey. And most importantly, I've learned it's okay to let light back into your life after loss.

Journal Prompts:

1. Think about how your relationship with your pet's memory has evolved since their death. What positive changes or personal growth have you experienced as a result of your grief journey?

2. Think about a small act of kindness someone has shown you during your grief journey. How did it impact you? How has it changed your perspective on support and understanding?

3. Describe a time when you caught yourself feeling joy after loss. What emotions surfaced, and how did you navigate them?

Chapter 10 –

❈

EMPOWERMENT THROUGH GRIEF

Journal Entry - November 16th, 2021

Christmas certainly is not my favourite time of year but I just deal with it. I'm excited to do Christmas Day on my own remembering the dogs doing all the things that I want to do maybe go to the beach, a walk, have a nice long bath, read, relax, have a glass of wine because I know I'll be with Steve for all of the other Christmases in the future I would hope. This is just going to be a Louise Christmas Day. I want it to be a day where I truly accept the trauma I went through and focus on the amazing bright future I have ahead of me and what happened to me was awful, tragic and that's okay. I really feel like the dogs could help me, their energy will really help me. I just feel that it's so magical.

Reading this entry now, I'm struck by how deeply I wanted to honour my dogs and my own needs during a typically challenging time of year. Christmas has never been easy for me, especially since my parents' divorce years ago. The pressure to provide extravagant gifts, prepare elaborate meals, and maintain a perfect facade often overshadows the true spirit of love and connection. For those of us who have lost a beloved pet, the holiday season can be particularly difficult. The absence of our animal companions is felt even more keenly during the festivities. It's okay to acknowledge this pain and to prioritise your own emotional well-being during this time. I've learned that it's crucial to listen to your own needs when grieving. For years, I sacrificed my own comfort to meet others' expectations during the holidays. But as I've been healing, I've realised the importance of setting boundaries and doing what feels right for me. It's not always easy to decline invitations or explain your choices to others, especially when they think they know what's best for you. But remember, you don't owe anyone an explanation for how you choose to spend your time, particularly when you're grieving. A simple "I have other plans" can be enough.

I encourage you to check in with yourself when faced with holiday invitations or expectations. Pay attention to how your body reacts. Do you feel tension or anxiety? Or do you feel a sense of peace? Trust these physical cues to guide your decisions. It's okay to take time to think about what you truly want and need. You might feel differently from one day to the next, and that's perfectly normal when you're grieving. Take care of yourself with tenderness and allow space for your emotions to ebb and flow. Whether your loss is recent or happened years ago, your grief is equal to the strength of the extremely close bond you held with your pet. There's no timeline for healing, and it's okay if certain times of year remain difficult. What matters most is that you honour your feelings and your pet's memory in whatever way feels right to you. As I write this, I'm reminded of the power of connecting with others who understand the depth of pet loss grief. Remember, it's okay to create new traditions and it's natural to feel their absence deeply, especially during the holidays.

Journal Entry – December 18th, 2021

I finally feel like I have some acceptance of the dogs' deaths. I now truly know and accept that those were the years I was meant to have with the dogs and they were both there to teach me so much. I still see robins all the time. I do feel their energy sometimes and now I know that their energy and love is still in my heart and I can access that whenever I need to.

This journal entry marked a turning point for me. It was the day I realised I had begun to feel a sense of acceptance regarding the deaths of my dogs. I finally understood that the years I had with them were exactly the years I was meant to have. They were there to teach me so much, and even now, I still see robins everywhere, little signs that remind me of their presence. Sometimes, I feel their energy so strongly, and it comforts me to know that their love and spirit are still within my heart. I can access that love whenever I need to. That entry was short and simple, but its significance lies in the word "acceptance." Acceptance is such a powerful yet challenging concept, especially when you're at the beginning of your grief journey. My heart goes out to anyone navigating those early days because I know how hard it is. But I also want you to know that reaching a place of acceptance is possible. For me, acceptance doesn't mean forgetting or being okay with what happened, it means finding peace with it. It means being able to sit with the discomfort of loss and still feel at ease with life as it is now.

For me, acceptance looked like fewer panic attacks and less overwhelming trauma. The deep wound of grief didn't disappear overnight, it still gets triggered sometimes, but it began to heal slowly. Acceptance came when I understood that the time my dogs were in my life was exactly what it was meant to be. That realisation was incredibly difficult for me because I struggled so much with the idea that they were gone too soon. I kept asking myself why, why did they have to die? Why wasn't I ready? Why now? My life had revolved around my dogs, they were my purpose, my everything. It felt so unfair that they were taken from me. I questioned everything, the universe, fate, because none of it made sense. All I wanted was my life back the way it used to be. But slowly, as time passed, I began to see signs, robins appearing in unexpected places, and sharp gusts of wind when I was thinking of the dogs or asking them for help when I was out walking. Those signs became a part of my acceptance. They reminded me that my dogs' love and energy were still with me, no matter where I was. At first, I believed their energy was tied to the house where they died, but over time, I realised that wasn't true. Their presence wasn't confined to one place, it was with me wherever I went. Whether I was at home, traveling through Ireland, or visiting friends, those little signs would appear. Those moments reassured me that their love hadn't left me.

Acceptance is such a layered experience it's not something you arrive at all at once. For me, it came in pieces, through memories, through signs, and through understanding that their love is always accessible in my heart. When anniversaries or birthdays come around and grief resurfaces, I find comfort in looking through scrapbooks, watching videos of them on my phone, or simply visualising their faces. These things help me focus on the joy they brought into my life rather than just the pain of their absence. I've also come to believe that out of great loss can come something new, a gift or an opportunity we couldn't have anticipated. This belief has been reinforced by stories from others who've experienced profound loss and found unexpected blessings afterward. For me, this new chapter has been about helping others navigate their grief journeys. It's important for me to share this because acceptance isn't something we're often taught to embrace when it comes to loss. Society tells us to bury our grief and move on, to live with it rather than truly process it. Before I started doing this personal grief work, I believed that too. I thought acceptance wasn't possible, that you just had to push your feelings down and keep going until another loss came along and you repeated the cycle. But now I know better. Acceptance isn't about erasing grief, it's about making space for it while also allowing yourself to heal and grow around it. If you're reading this and feeling stuck in your own grief, whether it's for a pet, a loved one, or any kind of loss, I want you to know that you're not alone. Everyone's journey is unique.

For me, accepting the deaths of Ozzie and Moose happened at different times because my relationships with them were so different. Ozzie had been with me for nearly nine years, we moved countries together, he saw me through breakups and major life changes. Moose was only with me for a shorter time but brought immense joy and taught me patience and compassion in ways Ozzie hadn't. Processing their losses couldn't happen simultaneously because each relationship was distinct. What helped me most during this journey was allowing myself to feel everything fully, the pain, the anger, the confusion, and then slowly finding ways to honour their memories while moving forward with my life. Writing down my thoughts helped me untangle the complicated emotions surrounding their deaths and in turn finding some acceptance. Acceptance might feel impossible right now if you're in the depths of sorrow, but trust me when I say it's within reach. It doesn't mean forgetting or letting go, it means carrying your love for them forward in a way that brings peace instead of pain. And if I could find my way there after feeling like I'd never see light again, you can too. Grief is not linear, grieving takes time, and however long it takes is okay.

Journal Entry – December 26th, 2021

What a day yesterday was. I finally got to do all the things I wanted to do on Christmas Day. I woke up in my own house, on my own and I did a nice meditation and I drove up the coast to the cliffs which was amazing. I was the only one at the cliffs and it was only lightly raining. I whispered to Ozzie and Moose and thanked them for always helping me. I felt at peace there. The cliff walk was a little busier with some people but still nice all the same. I had a lovely short video call with my best friend and seeing her face warmed my soul. I came home, I lit a fire, I built a mountain of cushions in front of the fire and I watched a little bit of Netflix. I had a lovely starter, a lovely main and a dessert for dinner. I went for a walk later that evening and I watched a movie before going up to bed to read my book and then had an hour long phone call with my amazing boyfriend. The day was perfect for me. I felt empowered, free, independent, peaceful and liberated. I always thought I didn't like being alone but now I actually do. I value time alone doing the things that make me happy and content. I am now more comfortable being alone with my thoughts. I have less anxiety. Nature heals and cleanses and having that in my life is a blessing in itself.

Looking back on this entry, I'm struck by the raw honesty and the unexpected joy I found in solitude. I had always believed that Christmas was a time for family gatherings, that being alone on such a day would be terribly sad. But this experience taught me otherwise. It was one of the most memorable days I can recall in recent years, peaceful, relaxing, and free from expectations. I must admit, I wasn't entirely forthcoming with everyone about my plans. The fear of judgment and shame was still a powerful force in my life at that time. Only my best friend and boyfriend knew the truth. It's a struggle I've since overcome, but back then, the thought of others' reactions weighed heavily on me. What made this day truly special was the connection I felt with Ozzie and Moose.

As I stood on the cliffs, whispering to them and feeling the sudden gusts of wind, I couldn't help but wonder if it was their way of embracing me. Some might call it imaginative thinking, but if it brings comfort and closeness to our lost companions, isn't that what matters most? This solitary Christmas taught me the value of putting my needs first, something that's often challenging for those of us navigating the waters of pet loss grief. We're so used to caring for others, our pets, our families, our friends, that we forget to care for ourselves. But how can we possibly tend to others if we're running on empty?

I've come to see that day as a gift I gave myself, a day of self-compassion and self-love. It's a practice I now encourage in others, especially those working through the grief of losing a beloved pet. You don't have to wait for Christmas or any special occasion. Give yourself permission to have a "me" day, whether it's planned to the minute or completely spontaneous. The emotions I experienced that day, empowerment, freedom, independence, peace, liberation, were profound. It was a day when I honoured the memory of my dogs, connected with nature, and did exactly what I wanted to do. In doing so, I found a strength I didn't know I possessed. I share this story not to overshadow those who find themselves involuntarily alone or working during the holidays. Rather, I hope it serves as an inspiration to value your time alone, to become comfortable with your thoughts, and to let go of the fear of judgment from others. Their opinions are often more a reflection of themselves than of you. In the end, this experience taught me that grief, like healing, is a deeply personal journey. There's no one-size-fits-all approach. Sometimes, the most powerful steps we can take are the ones that feel a little scary, a little unconventional. But in taking them, we often find exactly what we need, peace, connection, and a renewed sense of self.

Journal Prompts:

1. Reflect on a holiday tradition you shared with your pet. How might you honour their memory while creating a new tradition for yourself this year?

2. Reflect on a moment when you felt a sense of acceptance about your pet's death. What triggered this feeling, and how did it change your perspective on grief?

3. Reflect on a time when you chose solitude over company. How did it make you feel, and what did you learn about yourself in those moments of quiet?

Chapter 11 –

THE PATH TO SELF-COMPASSION

The end of 2021 had arrived, and I sat down with my journal to reflect on the past two years. This notebook had become a safe haven for all my emotions—sadness, trauma, anxiety, happiness, hope, joy, and love. It was a roller coaster of experiences that had shaped me into a stronger person. As I wrote that final entry on December 31st, I couldn't help but feel immense gratitude for how far I had come.

Journal Entry – December 31st, 2021

The end of 2021 has arrived. I started writing in this notebook two years ago. This notebook is full of sadness, trauma, anxiety, happiness, hope, joy, and love, a complete roller coaster. I can say I have emerged a stronger person after enduring it all. Steve has made the last eleven months incredible, helping me through my grief and anxiety while loving me unconditionally. My two beautiful dogs gifted me with this man. Wow, what a lucky girl I am. I am proud of myself for getting therapy and for holding strong boundaries in certain situations in my life. Also, I know there is still some trauma in my body, I know that, but that's okay. The panic attacks are few and far between now, and the anxiety isn't as crippling. I still miss them the exact same amount. I just... I'm able to deal with it a little better, and I'm more gentle and compassionate with myself. I know in my soul that my two angels will be by my side to help me with the journey in 2022 ahead. I will always love you, Ozzie and Moose. Stay close.

When I finished writing that entry and turned the page, something extraordinary happened, it was the very last page of the journal. It wasn't just the end of a year, it felt like the closing of a chapter in my life. On that final page, I wrote a small note to myself:

I hereby leave any trauma and pain from the past two years on this page. I choose now to move forward and open a new chapter of my life.

Reading it back now feels so profound, like a promise to myself that actually came true. That intention carried me into 2022 with hope and determination to heal further. Looking back at that journal entry now reminds me how much growth can come from grief if we allow ourselves to feel everything fully, the sadness and the joy alike. Steve, my partner, had been my rock. His unwavering love and support helped me navigate the depths of grief and anxiety. In many ways, I always felt that my two beautiful dogs, Ozzie and Moose, had gifted me with this incredible man. It was as if they were still looking out for me from beyond. Their love had brought me to therapy and taught me to set boundaries, something I never thought I'd be able to do.

I acknowledged that some trauma still lingered within me. Panic attacks were rear, and my anxiety no longer held the same crippling power over me. Though I missed Ozzie and Moose just as much as ever, I had learned to be more compassionate and gentle with myself. Deep down, I knew they were still by my side, guiding me into the year ahead. Ozzie and Moose's love didn't end when they died, it transformed into something that continues to guide me every day. Their lives taught me courage, vulnerability, and the importance of honouring every emotion. If you're grieving the loss of a beloved pet right now, know this, your grief matters and is so important. Go easy on yourself as you navigate this journey. Write letters to your pet if it helps, tell them about your day or share your memories with them. Their love never truly leaves you, it stays close in ways you might not always see but can always feel. Ozzie and Moose gave me so many gifts, gifts that continue to shape my life in ways I never could have imagined. And for that, I will always be grateful.

Journal Entry – January 15th, 2022

I just got home from a 2-hour acupuncture appointment. I feel super chill and relaxed lying here on the bed. My acupuncturist said that the tight muscles in my neck might have been the cause of the vertigo attacks and possibly stress. I know myself that I'm not managing my stress levels very well so I will just have to prioritise 'me time'. During the appointment

I was able to empty my mind somewhat. The only thoughts that kept coming in were of the dogs. I imagined Oz under my left hand and Moose under my right hand. I could feel myself lightly rubbing Bob's soft fluffy part of his velvet ears and lightly stroking him with my finger down between his eyes to his nose. He loved when I did that and found it relaxing. Moose just wanted to be near me. She never often looked to be touched. She felt comfort just being beside me. A few flashbacks of their death and burial came in and out of my mind which brought a few tears but that's okay. I tried to interrupt those thoughts with the joy that I experienced with them. I do need to do some more healing. I'm not quite there yet. There's no rush, no rush for healing, no rush to start the business, just go easy on myself and all will fall into place when it should as it should. I still have some learning to do. You work full-time Louise. Change takes time. My acupuncturist said when I feel overwhelmed and stressed just to have compassion for myself and say 'I am aware of what my path is and things are changing slowly at a pace that's comfortable for me. All will be well.' I need to stop with all this pressure, all the pressure I put on myself. One thing at a time. There is no deadline. The universe and the angels will guide me in the right directions. Trust your intuition always. Love you Oz and moose.

This entry takes me back to a challenging time in my life. I was battling severe vertigo attacks, which I later discovered were a form of vestibular migraine. These episodes were debilitating, leaving me unable to function normally for days at a time. In hindsight, I believe these physical symptoms were closely tied to the intense grief and stress I was experiencing. During my acupuncture sessions, I found solace in visualising my beloved dogs. I could almost feel Ozzie's velvety ears beneath my fingertips and imagine Moose's comforting presence beside me. These moments of connection, even if only in my mind, brought both comfort and tears. It's important to note that Ozzie had many nicknames, including Bob. He would come running whenever I used this loving nickname, highlighting the special bond we shared. Moose, on the other hand, was more independent but always liked to be near me, finding comfort in my presence without necessarily seeking physical touch.

As I read this entry now, I'm struck by how much healing I still had ahead of me at that point. It's a reminder that grief is not a linear process, and it's okay to take the time you need. I was learning to be gentler with myself, to stop putting so much pressure on my own shoulders. My acupuncturist's advice resonates deeply with me even now: have compassion for yourself, trust that things are changing at a pace that's right for you, and believe that all will be well. This guidance helped me navigate the overwhelming emotions and physical symptoms I was experiencing. Looking back, I realise that my grief was manifesting in various ways, through panic attacks, PTSD flashbacks, and these debilitating vertigo episodes. It was as if my body was forcing me to confront the emotions I had been suppressing. This experience taught me the importance of allowing ourselves to feel and process our grief, rather than pushing it aside. For those of you who may be experiencing physical symptoms related to your grief, know that this is not uncommon. Our physical bodies often carry the weight of our emotional pain. Seeking support, whether through therapy, a medical professional, alternative treatments like acupuncture, or simply talking to loved ones, can be crucial in navigating this difficult journey. Be patient with yourself, just as I learned to be patient with myself. Trust your intuition, allow yourself to feel, and know that it's okay to take things one day at a time. Your journey of healing is uniquely yours, and it's valid in all its forms.

Journal Entry – January 27th, 2022

Still a tough month but doing meditations and focusing on what's good in my life is helping me to get through it somewhat. Yesterday I had a good therapy session, I told her about the panic attack I had on St Stephen's day when Steve and I had to go to visit his family. I felt quite trapped and alone when he had to leave for a work call because there was two dogs in the house. I knew that I was stuck there and I had no way of leaving and the anxiety set in and when he returned a few hours later I had a panic attack in the car on the way home. We spoke about it and the therapist said that I need to leave a delay in the narrative and story of what happened and just say to Steve "I'm anxious" with a full stop. Basically just label the feeling and sit with it without following on with the narrative to try and avoid it turning into a panic attack. Do whatever I need to do to calm my nervous system in that moment, deep breathing, squeezing a ball of blu tack, use my the ring that's on my finger (it's a spinner ring), the roller ball essential oils to smell or rub it on my temples. Then, later on talk about the emotions and feelings in more detail. I am not holding it in, I am just delaying telling the story as my focus is calming my nervous system in that moment. It really helped talking that through. So I'm going to try

*and do more de-stressing because I know it's needed. This weekend I want
to spend more time in nature.*

This entry captures a pivotal moment in my healing journey.
The strategy my therapist suggested, simply labelling the
feeling without diving into the narrative, became a powerful
tool for managing my anxiety and preventing panic attacks. It's
not about suppressing emotions, but rather prioritising
calming our nervous system in triggering moments. After
losing both of my dogs, I found myself in numerous situations
that triggered intense emotions. It's natural to experience these
feelings during grief, but it's crucial not to be hard on yourself.
Remember, you've been through a traumatic loss. Your pet was
your world, your purpose, your family, your best friend, and
the source of unconditional love and comfort. Losing all of
that is undeniably traumatic. While this strategy helped me, it's
important to recognise that everyone's grief journey is unique.
Whether you experience panic attacks, severe anxiety,
inconsolable sadness, or depression, the key is to find ways to
regulate your nervous system. This might involve deep
breathing exercises, using a spinner ring, smelling essential oils,
or any other technique that helps ground you in the present
moment.

Grounding techniques are powerful tools for managing
anxiety, stress, grief and panic attacks by helping individuals
reconnect with the present moment. These techniques work
by engaging the senses and redirecting focus away from

distressing thoughts or emotions. There are many types of grounding techniques, but here are a few to consider:

- The 5-4-3-2-1 technique: Identify 5 things you can see, 4 things you can touch, 3 things you can hear, 2 things you can smell, and 1 thing you can taste.

- Using water: Take a shower or run your hands under a stream of water to focus on the sensory experience.

- Holding ice: The intense cold sensation can quickly shift your attention.

- Recite a mantra: Something simple like "I am safe, I am present."

- Listen to grounding music: Something calming or steady.

- Say the alphabet backwards: It forces focus and redirects your mind.

- Progressive muscle relaxation: Tense and relax each muscle group in your body.

- Touch something comforting: Focus on its texture, weight, and temperature, for example squeezing a stress ball, or holding a sentimental item.

- Hug yourself: Wrap your arms around your body for comfort.

- Perform simple movements: Wiggle your toes, stretch your arms, or rotate your neck.

Grounding techniques are effective because they interrupt the cycle of anxiety or panic by shifting focus to immediate sensory input. This helps calm the nervous system and promotes mindfulness. Regular practice can improve overall emotional regulation and mental health. It's important to note that different techniques may work better for different people. Experimenting with various methods and practicing them regularly, even when not in distress, can help you find the most effective techniques for your needs and make them more accessible during moments of high anxiety or panic. It's okay to delay telling the story of your grief. Focus on calming yourself first, then return to those emotions when you feel more regulated. This approach allows you to process your feelings more effectively and may even help you gain new insights into your grief. As you navigate your pet loss journey, be compassionate towards yourself. It's normal to want to avoid triggering situations, but prolonged avoidance can hinder the grieving process. Consider gradual exposure to environments that remind you of your pet, always ensuring you have the option to leave if needed.

Journal Prompts:

1. Imagine you're writing the last page of your grief journal. What message would you leave for yourself as you close this chapter and move forward, while still honouring your pet's memory?

2. Reflect on a time when your grief manifested physically. How did you cope with these symptoms, and what did they teach you about your emotional state?

3. Reflect on a moment when you felt overwhelmed by grief for your pet. How did your body and mind react? Write about any techniques you used (or wish you had known about) to help ground yourself in that moment

Chapter 12 –

FINDING PURPOSE IN PAIN

Journal Entry – July 8th, 2022

I focus on the good in my life now. I've signed up to do the grief recovery specialist training in August, and hopefully by the end of the year, I will have a website and social media ready to launch my business. I am so, so determined and excited for my new life. I have outgrown my job now, it's clear that it's just paying the bills. I know that I am definitely an introvert, I'm not a social butterfly. I like my own company and am perfectly happy doing my own thing. I do miss my dogs still. Last week was particularly bad, I cried a lot. And I'll be crying a lot when I do this training in August, but it will help.

Looking back at this entry now feels surreal, it's as though it was written by a version of me who was planting the seeds of everything that has since blossomed in my life. At that point, I had already signed up for the Grief Recovery Institute's training program because their approach intrigued me so much. They didn't just recognise pet loss as valid, they offered tools specifically designed for it. When I first stumbled upon their website during one of my many late-night internet searches, it felt like fate. The site kept popping up no matter what keywords I used, and eventually, I couldn't ignore it anymore. The idea of learning how to heal myself and maybe even helping others began as a fleeting thought but quickly grew into something much bigger. I remember sitting on my couch with tears streaming down my face, laptop open on my lap as I searched desperately for help. Surely, I thought, there had to be others out there who felt this same deep pain after losing their pets. Surely, there were others who felt as lost and broken as I did. That realisation, that there must be others like me was the first spark of what would later become my mission.

When I finally had a consultation call with someone from the Grief Recovery Institute, they asked me why I wanted to join their program. My answer was simple: "I want to feel better." It was such a relief to have someone validate that what I was experiencing was real grief, deep and profound and that it deserved recognition and support. But they also told me something else, before helping others, I would need to do my own grief work first. That scared me because it meant confronting feelings I had been suppressing for far too long. Yet deep down, I knew that this was exactly what I needed, not just for myself but for anyone else who might one day turn to me for guidance. Reflecting on this journey now, years later, fills me with gratitude, not just for how far I've come but for what Ozzie and Moose have given me even after their deaths. Their deaths were unimaginably painful, but they also gifted me with clarity and purpose: a new career helping others navigate their own losses, a new relationship filled with love, and even a new home where healing could truly begin. If you're reading this and wondering what your pet might have gifted you, even amidst your grief, I encourage you to sit quietly with that thought or journal about it. It doesn't have to be something big, sometimes the smallest shifts can have the most profound impact. Ozzie and Moose gave me more than just memories, they left behind precious gifts that still shape my life in the most beautiful ways each and every day. I will forever be grateful for that.

Journal Entry – August 1st, 2022

Two weeks ago on the 16th of July 2022 I cycled and completed a 120km leisure cycle. I wanted to write about it as it was such a huge moment in my life. I completed it 3 years ago too, but this time my two friends couldn't make it so I cycled it on my own. Obviously there were a couple of hundred people there but I say I was on my own as I didn't know anybody else doing it. Steve was driving the route, helping me along the way. I wouldn't have been able to finish it without his support. I really noticed how fit I was and all the training had paid off. I felt like the dogs were in it with me too, keeping me going all along the way. I think that day for me was so magical because it proved the saying: "you can do anything you put your mind to". It's a day I will look back on and lock into my memory.

This entry, though brief, captures a special moment in my journey through grief. It was the first major cycling event I'd undertaken since losing my beloved dogs, and I found myself reaching out to them in spirit as I pedalled along. With each challenging hill, I'd silently ask for their strength, feeling their presence with me every kilometre of the way. I'm no professional athlete, just an amateur cyclist with a spinning bike at home. But as I pushed myself through those long hours of solitary cycling, I discovered a resilience I didn't know I possessed. It was as if my dogs were there, urging me forward, helping me prove to myself that I could do hard things even in the midst of grief. This experience taught me that it's okay, even beneficial to set goals and work towards achievements while grieving. It doesn't mean you're forgetting your pet or moving on too quickly. Instead, it can be a way of honouring their memory and the strength they gave you. I found myself talking to my dogs throughout the cycle, asking for their support and guidance. Some might find this silly, but I believe it's a beautiful way to maintain that spiritual connection with our departed pets. Whether it's during a challenging physical feat, a job interview, or just a tough day, calling on that bond can provide comfort and strength.

Grief is not a structured journey, and it affects everyone differently. The pain I felt losing my dogs was far more intense than what I'd experienced with human losses earlier in my life. This surprised me, but I've come to understand that the unique bond we form with our pets, that daily, intimate, non-verbal connection, creates a profound type of love that, when lost, leaves an equally profound void. If you're grieving, please know that it's okay to feel overwhelmed, confused, or surprised by the intensity of your emotions. Your grief is valid, no matter how it compares to other losses you may have experienced. Remember, your life doesn't have to come to a complete standstill because your pet has died. Take all the time you need to grieve, but know that when you're ready, it's okay to start moving forward again. Your pet's love and the relationship you shared can be a source of strength as you face new challenges and set new goals. Your pet may no longer be physically present, but the love you shared and the lessons they taught you will always be a part of who you are. Whether you're taking on a physical challenge like a long cycle, starting a new job, or simply getting through a difficult grief day, know that your pet's spirit can still be with you, cheering you on and giving you strength. In the end, grief is a testament to the depth of our love. By allowing ourselves to grieve fully and then gradually re-engage with life, we honour the profound impact our pets have had on our lives. They may be gone from our sight, but they live on in our hearts and our souls, continuing to inspire and support us in ways we might never have imagined.

Journal Entry – August 28th, 2022

I've been really missing the dogs lately. I would give anything to be able to hug them and even to rub Ozzie's velvet ears. I do feel a lot better after completing the grief recovery method process, working on an estranged relationship with a family member and working on the relationships I shared with my dogs. It was difficult, but I do feel a difference. I feel more calm and at peace about it. It's an amazing program. I cannot wait to start my business. It's going to be amazing, I know it. I have somebody helping me design a website. I've been designing social media posts, and that will be a massive help. It's full steam ahead, and I've never been more sure about something than I have about this career move. It's a full-body yes, and my intuition is guiding me. It's never sent me wrong before, and everything is as it's supposed to be right now. I am blessed and lucky to be in the position I am in right now. I need to focus on that but also communicating my feelings. Say the things that make me feel uncomfortable. That's how we grow.

Reflecting on this journal entry now, I see how far I've come. The Grief Recovery Method® was transformative for me. As someone fully certified in this program, I've seen its power firsthand, not just in helping others but also in healing myself. While my focus is on pet loss recovery, the program is versatile and can be applied to many forms of grief. In fact, before addressing the loss of my beloved dogs, I was encouraged to work on a human relationship that had caused me pain for years. That process wasn't easy. For three years, I had carried anger and unresolved grief over that relationship. Therapy and conversations with friends had helped to some extent, but nothing provided the clarity and release that the structured steps of this program did. Through written exercises and guided reflections, I was able to let go of so much anger. By the end of it, the pain that had once felt so sharp had dulled into something manageable, something freeing. This experience reinforced my belief in the importance of taking action in grief recovery. The program challenged me to sit with my pain, to face it head-on rather than burying it. And while it was hard work, some days excruciating, it was worth every moment because it brought me peace. Now, when I think about Ozzie and Moose, the ache is still there but softened by gratitude for the love we shared. Their memory doesn't bring panic or overwhelming sadness anymore, instead, it reminds me of how deeply they enriched my life.

As I wrote in my journal, learning to communicate openly has been another key part of this journey. For so long, I silenced myself to avoid conflict or discomfort, a habit born from years of people-pleasing. But through therapy and self-reflection, I've come to understand that speaking my truth is essential for genuine relationships. This lesson has been especially important in navigating grief for a pet, an experience that is often misunderstood or dismissed by others. When someone makes an insensitive comment like "You can just get another dog," it takes courage to respond honestly: "That's not helpful for me right now. My pet was irreplaceable." Speaking up in these moments isn't about being rude, it's about honouring our truth and the profound bond we shared with our pets. I've learned that even if someone doesn't understand or validate our grief, what matters most is that we stand firm in our love and respect for our pets. Saying out loud how much they meant to us is an act of healing, a way of claiming their importance in our lives. If you're grieving a beloved pet and feeling unsupported by those around you, please know you're not alone. Many people struggle with this kind of disenfranchised grief, it's painful but valid nonetheless. When others fail to acknowledge your loss or abandon you in your time of need, it can feel devastating, but your feelings are real and deserve recognition. In those moments when the weight feels unbearable, try wrapping your arms around yourself as a gesture of self-compassion. Speak words of love and remembrance for your pet out loud, it may feel silly at first, but it can be incredibly comforting. Grief is a journey without a fixed timeline or destination. Be patient with yourself as you navigate its twists and turns. Remember that your bond with your pet was, and still is, beautiful beyond words.

Journal Prompts:

1. Think about an unexpected way your pet's death has changed your life or perspective. What new path, insight, or purpose has emerged from your grief journey?

2. Think of a goal or activity you've been reluctant to pursue since losing your pet. In what ways could taking this step honour your pet's memory?

3. Describe a time when you pushed yourself to communicate something uncomfortable. How did it help you grow, and what did you learn from the experience?

Chapter 13 –

CARRYING THEIR LOVE
FORWARD

Journal Entry – October 21st, 2022

I am starting my first online grief recovery method support group on Monday with three wonderful women. I'm super nervous but at the same time so excited and looking forward to changing my life. I can do it. I actually am surrendering to the universe's plans for me. Tomorrow is the 22nd of October, the 3-year anniversary of my two babies. I am feeling emotional this week and Steve and I are hoping to go to their favourite beach in memory of them, as we usually do. Their memory is driving me on to help others who have lost their pets. I just feel so compelled to help others. I really do. I just want to make some kind of difference in the world. My freedom is fast approaching and I am so impatient. I love the love from Ozzie and Moose because it's safely stored in my heart, where I can dip into it now and then when I need it.

Reflecting on that time now, it feels surreal to think about how far I've come since October 2022. My first support group was what I called my "pilot group." It was the first time I guided others through the Grief Recovery Method®, and despite being fully prepared, I was filled with nerves. But those weeks with those three women were transformative. Their willingness to share their stories and trust me with their grief gave me the confidence to move forward and officially launch my business. Their testimonials meant so much to me that they were among the first things I shared on my website once it was completed. I felt an immense sense of pride, not just in myself but in the work we had done together. That week wasn't just about starting something new, it was also about honouring the past. The day after writing that journal entry, Steve and I went to the beach that my dogs loved so much. A yearly ritual on their anniversary, a day dedicated entirely to remembering them and celebrating the unique relationships I shared with both of them. It's a tradition that brings me peace and connection, one that I plan to continue for as long as it feels right.

If there's one thing I've learned through this journey, it's the importance of finding ways to keep your pet's memory alive in a way that feels meaningful to you. Whether it's visiting a special place, creating art, or simply sitting quietly with your thoughts, these rituals can be incredibly healing. And if you choose not to share those moments with anyone else, that's okay too, grief is deeply personal, and there's no right or wrong way to navigate it. As I look back on those early days of starting my support groups and building my business, I'm reminded of how much love and determination can grow from loss. The memory of Ozzie and Moose continues to guide me every step of the way, pushing me to connect with others who feel alone in their grief. Their love is a constant presence in my life, A steady source of strength I can access at any time. If you are struggling with your own loss, know that you're not in this alone. The pain is real and valid, but so is the love you carry for your pet. It's stored safely within you, ready to be accessed whenever you need comfort or strength. Close your eyes and imagine dipping into that reservoir of love, it's always there for you. This chapter of my life taught me that even in the depths of grief, there is room for growth and connection. It showed me that our pets' legacies can live on through the ways we choose to honour them and help others. And most importantly, it reminded me that love, whether shared with a person or a pet, is never truly lost, it simply changes form and continues to exist within us forever.

In the depths of winter, as December 2022 arrived, I found myself at a turning point. For years, this month had been one I dreaded, but this time felt different. I was on the cusp of launching my new business, Light After Loss, and a sense of empowerment, excitement, and hope filled me. With my website nearly complete and systems in place, I was ready to embark on this new journey. The support I received from fellow pet loss professionals warmed my heart, affirming that I was on the right path.

Journal Entry – December 1st, 2022

Welcome December, the month I have hated for years but this year feels different. I'm about to launch my brand new business Light After Loss. I'm feeling so empowered, excited and hopeful. The website is all but finished and I've sorted all my systems and calendars and figured out everything I need to put into place. I have two weeks left until my first pilot group is complete and I did a wonderful mindset workshop and it's just really empowered me. I got some really lovely supportive messages from other pet loss professionals which felt really good. It feels like a full body yes that's all I know. 2023 is going to be a magical year in so many ways and I'm very impatient, I can't wait!

This entry marked an important milestone in my journey through grief. Looking back at earlier entries, I could see how far I'd come since losing both my beloved dogs. The overwhelming emotions and struggles I faced in the beginning had gradually given way to a sense of hope that had been quietly growing beneath the surface. While life would never be the same without my companions, I discovered that there was a way to embrace my new self and my new life. The connection with my pets remained strong, even if only in spirit. I found comfort in reaching out to them when I needed strength or love, believing that our bond transcended the physical world.

My transformation from a grieving pet parent to a business owner supporting others through their loss was unexpected but organic. It grew from my pain, much like how other challenging life experiences can sometimes lead to positive growth. I encourage you to look closely at your own life and see if you can identify any magical or positive outcomes that have emerged from difficult times. I share my journey to offer hope to those at any stage of their pet loss experience. Whether you're in the darkest depths of grief or starting to see glimmers of light, know that healing is possible. It doesn't mean forgetting your pet or diminishing their importance in your life. Instead, it's about finding new ways to honour their memory and carry their love forward.

In the early days after losing Ozzie and Moose, I experienced incredibly dark thoughts. The emptiness of the house and the loss of my daily routines centred around them, left me feeling lost and alone. There were moments when I questioned how I could go on without them. If you've had similar thoughts, please know that you're not alone and that it's okay to feel this way. However, it's crucial to share these feelings with trusted individuals who can support you. As time passed, I began to see a faint glimmer of light, almost as if Ozzie and Moose were shining it down on me, encouraging me to reach for it. It wasn't easy to grasp at first, but slowly, I found the strength to pull myself out of that pit of despair. This hope, this light, became my lifeline. I started to imagine my dogs guiding me towards new experiences and opportunities. They led me to a wonderful new relationship and inspired me to create a business to help others through pet loss. As I opened myself to these positive changes, I found the darkness receding.

If you're struggling, try to visualise your pet helping to pull you up, encouraging you to get out of bed, or guiding you to their favourite places. Honour their memory by following these gentle nudges, even if tears still flow. It's all part of the grieving process and the journey towards healing. Remember, there is light after loss. It may seem impossible to see at first, but it's there, waiting for you to reach out and grasp it. Let your pet guide you towards healing and new beginnings. Be patient with yourself, journal your feelings, connect with others who understand, and don't be afraid to seek support when you need it. Practice self-care as you navigate these grief waves, and know that hope is always there, even in the darkest of times.

Journal Entry – December 24th, 2022

Well, the year is nearly over. It's been a tough month and a fun month, all thrown in one. I have had extremely bad anxiety, and that's been really difficult. But that being said, my dogs are always guiding me on this incredible path. This new path for 2023 is going to be so different, so inspiring, so fulfilling, and I know it. I know it with all my soul. Their healing energy is always keeping me focused on my dreams to raise as much awareness about pet loss as I possibly can and help as many grieving pet parents as I possibly can. I know deep down I can do it. From the pain I suffered will come motivation to help others, others that are in the position I once was. My new life is just around the corner. It's within reach now. Those three beautiful, brave ladies were the beginning, and I am confident. I am capable. I am ready. I love you both with everything I am. Thank you for guiding me in the right direction.

As I look back on this entry now, I'm struck by the mixture of pain and hope that filled my heart. The anxiety that had gripped me so tightly was still present, but alongside it was a growing sense of purpose. My beloved dogs, though no longer physically with me, were guiding me towards a new chapter in my life. It's been quite a journey since I started writing in my journals, I'm amazed at how far I've come and how much I've shared. This particular journal entry marks a significant moment in my healing process. For the first time, I felt comfortable sharing the way I used to sign off my entries, with a message of love to my dogs. It's a small thing, perhaps, but it represents a big step in my willingness to be vulnerable and open about my grief. In this entry, I mention "those three beautiful, brave ladies." They were the first clients in my pilot group for the Grief Recovery Method® program. These women, who had never done anything like this before, trusted me to guide them through their own grief journeys. They hold a special place in my heart, as they marked the beginning of my small business dedicated to helping others through pet loss.

Looking back, I can see how my ability to connect with my dogs' memory and energy had grown. In the early days after their deaths, I was trapped in a cycle of replaying their final days, unable to feel anything but emptiness and numbness. I felt stuck in time, going through the motions of daily life while inside, I was frozen in grief. To those of you who might be feeling this way now, please know that it's normal. Grief can manifest in many ways, social anxiety, a lack of purpose, trouble concentrating, deep sadness, hopelessness, panic attacks, and even PTSD. These are all common responses to the profound loss of a beloved pet. Treat yourself with kindness as you navigate these difficult emotions.

As time passed and I learned more about grief, sought support, and went through the Grief Recovery Method® myself, I began to experience fewer symptoms. This gradual improvement gives me hope, and I want to share that hope with you. These painful responses don't last forever, but it's crucial to give yourself space to grieve. I've learned that our bodies often cry out for us to sit still and feel our grief. It's tempting to run from the pain, to distract ourselves with alcohol, binge-watching TV, or endlessly scrolling through our phones. But I've found that taking time to be quiet and present with our grief can be incredibly healing. Try this: go into your bedroom alone, close the door, and put away all screens and distractions. Place your hand on your heart and tune into what your body needs. You might find that emotions start to surface, that tears begin to flow. When this happens to me, I wrap my arms around myself and gently say, "It's okay. I'm safe." I speak to my broken heart, to every cell in my body that's carrying this grief. I reassure myself, I don't pressure myself or put myself down. I simply comfort myself for a few minutes.

This simple practice has been a comforting part of my healing journey. It might sound strange, but what do you have to lose by trying it? Even if you can only manage it for a few minutes a week, it can make a huge difference. I share all of this, my private thoughts, my personal practices, because I know how isolating pet loss can be. So many people face judgment or criticism when grieving a pet, and that's why I wrote this book. If sharing my experiences can make even one person feel less alone, then it's worth it. My journey hasn't been easy. I've faced hurtful comments from colleagues, family members, and strangers. But I've channelled that pain into my passion for helping others through pet loss. If you've received similar comments, know that you're not alone. Use that pain as fuel for something you're passionate about. I've been told I'm "too sensitive," but I've come to see my sensitivity as a superpower. It's what allows me to be empathetic, compassionate, and in touch with my emotions. If you've ever been told to "stop being so sensitive," I want you to know that your sensitivity is a beautiful, positive trait.

To you, the reader, I want to say thank you. You are brave. You are not alone. You are not crazy for grieving your pet. You deserve support, love, and comfort during this painful time of loss. As you move forward, remember that growth and new adventures are possible, even after devastating loss. As we come to the end of this journey together, I want to leave you with a message of hope. Your grief is unique and legitimate, and it is a testament to the deep love you shared with your pet. But remember, just as the seasons change, so too will your grief evolve. In the darkest moments, when the pain feels overwhelming, know that you are not alone. Thousands of others have walked this path before you, and thousands more walk it alongside you now. Your sensitivity, your ability to love so deeply, is not a weakness, it's a beautiful strength that will guide you through this difficult time. As you move forward, go easy on yourself. Honor your grief by giving it space to breathe. Take those quiet moments to connect with your heart, to listen to what your soul needs. And when you're ready, let the love you shared with your pet inspire you to new heights, new passions, new ways of connecting with the world around you.

Remember, healing is not about forgetting. It's about finding a way to carry your wonderful pet's memory with you, allowing their love to continue shaping your life in positive ways. Your pet's physical presence may be gone, but the bond you shared is eternal. As you close this book, know that you have within you the strength to navigate this loss. Your journey of healing may not be straightforward, and that's okay. Take it one day at a time, and trust that brighter days lie ahead. Your pet's love will always be a part of you, guiding you towards hope, healing, and new beginnings. You are amazing. You are resilient. And you are loved. May you find peace and comfort in the memories you cherish, and may your heart gradually open to the joy and love that still surrounds you. Your story doesn't end here, it's just beginning a new chapter.

Journal Prompts:

1. Imagine dipping into the reservoir of love you have for your pet. What does this feel like? Describe the sensations, emotions, and memories that surface.

2. Imagine your pet guiding you towards a positive change in your life. What would they encourage you to do or try?

3. Write a letter to your future self, one year from now. What words of encouragement and hope would you share about your journey through grief and healing?

ABOUT THE AUTHOR

Louise Griffey is a dedicated Pet Loss Support Specialist based in Ireland, trained in the Grief Recovery Method®. As the founder of Light After Loss, she offers compassionate online support to pet parents worldwide, helping them navigate the complex emotions associated with the loss of a beloved animal companion. Louise's expertise in pet loss grief has been featured on national television, radio, and in media publications. Through her work, including informative workshops, support programs, and "The Pet Loss Journals" podcast, Louise provides a beacon of hope for those experiencing the often overlooked but profound impact of pet loss. Her compassionate approach to grief has touched the lives of countless individuals, guiding them on their journey to healing and recovery. For those seeking further support, Louise's services and resources can be found at www.lightafterloss.ie.

Printed in Dunstable, United Kingdom